200 ~ DECLARED

~

Poems on the Run

200 ~ DECLARED

~

Poems on the Run

-o-o-o-

-o-o-o-

200 ~ DECLARED

~

Poems on the Run

-o-o-o-

To add to the poems published earlier in '*101 Daft Notions*' here are *99* new ones; a '*second innings*' so to speak.

The '*200~Declared*' are mostly light-hearted and spontaneous reflections on some of the pastimes and occupations we pursue in journeying through this rather mad life on the planet Earth. I guess they sprang forth in a stream of relative unconsciousness. Just a tiny bit of fun, I hope.

The new poems each have fourteen lines *(those marked with an asterisk*)* while the old ones have sixteen… don't ask me why.

-o-o-o-

I'm sure
there's a word
for it

Dan Tunnelly

To B - from D

with love as always

200 ~ Declared ~ *Poems on the Run*

Index by Page: *(for alphabetical index see page 202)*

Cricketer *(200 ~ Declared)* *

I'll throw my cap high in the air
I've scored two hundred, I declare
It saddens me now I must cease
It's my last innings at the crease

Last walk to the pavilion
No more my trusty pads to don
My English bat of willow weeps
And chronicles of matches keeps

A chain of ground has been my home
In yards that's twenty-two you know
Now sight screens at the boundary
Are bitter-sweet past memories

But on wet afternoons as these
My Wisden knows no boundaries

-o-o-o-

~ Out on Bails ~

1

Vet *(Low Target)*

The Practice of the vet was small
The animals must not be tall
The ceilings were all beamed and low
Alpacas yes, but llamas no

Shetland ponies were her limit
Horses just would not fit in it
Then one day a giraffe arrived
It lowered its head and in it dived

'My God,' she cried 'What shall we do?
It's stuck right fast as if with glue'
She pushed so hard, the owner pulled
They feared it might need to be culled

At last it popped right out again
Vet exhausted, owner drained
The vet cried 'Look, if you ask me
Girrafrica's where it should be'

-o-o-o-

~ Tall Tale Heart ~

Fairground Attendant *(Whirly Gigs)* *

On the Waltzers he would stand
Hobnail boots and grease-stained hands
Slicked back hair and drainpipe jeans
In the days of bygone dreams

Etherial atmosphere he crafted
Whirling music nightward wafted
On balmy evenings to and fro
As revellers did come and go

Here for everyone's delight
Don't be shy, don't stall tonight
Coconuts and fishes gold
Candyfloss like bouffants bold

Now, on latter-day adventures
He'd swing me fast, I'd loose my dentures

-o-o-o-

~ Out for a Spin ~

Ghostwriter *(That's the Spirit)*

Inside us all they say's a book
He opened up to have a look
And while he felt he wished to write
He couldn't get the syntax right

His grammar too was less than cool
Despite his time at grammar school
He called a friend to help him out
He needed aid without a doubt

The ghostwriter began to scrawl
He certainly had the wherewithal
Before the second month had passed
Appeared an almost finished draft

Mystery was the genre chose
The final chapter he'd not closed
The writer had just disappeared
He really was a ghost, how weird

-o-o-o-

~ Medium Font ~

Rhymer *(Thomas? Maybe Not)* *

I've tried to Sonnets Lumière
Can't guarantee the meter there
I'm what I am and nothing more
The iamb ain't what it is, for sure

Poetry that's classical
Can make a tale seem farcical
Accentual-syllabic verse
Constricts the tales, what could be worse?

Rhythm and rhyme my aim withal
Though purists might well be appalled
At least I've got the fourteen lines
But then I've made the pairs to rhyme

Though critics may be somewhat stumped
Pentameters can run and jump

-o-o-o-

~ Some Lines Dancing ~

5

Farmer *(Plough the Fields and Shatter)*

The land he's tilled these thousand years
Seems overwhelmed with floods of tears
The climate's changing that's for sure
The drains they just can take no more

The food we eat depends on him
Yet we throw lots into the bin
We want him to plant trees instead
But that won't keep the mouths all fed

Dilemma and dichotomy
Woods for trees we cannot see
Are flocks and herds extravagant?
A diet based on naught but plants?

An idea's seed is what we need
The added billions best to feed
Stacking plants all one-on-one
For stacks of people... that's job done

-o-o-o-

~ Do You Dig It? ~

Transport Café Owner *(Well Toasted)* *

Her Portakabin café she loves
The ambiance fits like a glove
The bacon, sausage and baked beans
Suit every lorry driver's dreams

Her fried eggs are the best for miles
Engendering lots of truckers' smiles
And as for tea, it's served in buckets
Posher venues can't quite truck it

Queues mount up so she's expanding
Four more cabins recent landing
No drivers seem to want to work
For breakfast they're prepared to shirk

Their welcome they all overstay
With mushroom on the motorway

-o-o-o-

~ Fry-up Their Street ~

Poet *(A Reason for Rhyme)*

Stan's a poet down our way
Stanzas spilling out all day
There's gusto there in all his poems
Striding past his neighbours' homes

His brain is full of words you see
And they spill out for you and me
Down the pavement he will flit
Pouring out some daily wit

Sonnets on the paper punning
Haikus always agile running
Limericks if lines allow
Couplets more succinct somehow

When all's said and done in time
The sentiment will always rhyme
He keeps his word and gives it too
His wordy cause should see us through

-o-o-o-

~ On the Write Lines ~

Shoemaker *(Lost Soles)*

Those boots of his were made to last
He's worn that pair since ages past
He cobbled them himself you see
A shoemaker destined to be

His ancestors were crispins all
Boots and shoes since 'fore the fall
Adam must have known their names
As he donned footwear facing shame

Hand in hand with Eve he travelled
Around the time the world unravelled
All the same, he needed boots
Thanks to that dread forbidden fruit

And Eve had slippers fine as well
Or blisters would have given her Hell
Now mankind wanders round and round
All's doomed and Hell for leather bound

-o-o-o-

~ Down at Heal ~

Boy Scout *(Dyb Dob)* *

Society once thought it good
Inspiring usefulness to bud
We all indulged in Bob-a-Jobbing
Hard-earned cash from folks a-robbing

To wash a car or sweep a yard
I'm sure we really did work hard
Just for some coppers in our mitt
Servitude, the benefit

But let loose lately we can't be
The dangers are all there to see
Cos safety's lacking at our age
And they won't pay the Living Wage

The kids' minds now must surely boggle
Asking 'What's a bloody woggle?'

-o-o-o-

~ Powell Sharing ~

God *(Day by Deity)*

God knows what he was thinking of
Creating hate alongside love
That serpent was a big mistake
Fangs again for not much, mate

The old gods they all mischief made
In roguery they worked and played
The Greeks, the Romans and the rest
With conflict they did us invest

But now we have new deities
The smartphones and the big TVs
Enchanting us both day and night
I wonder if it's really right

The conflict it still bubbles up
The hate it surfaces corrupt
But if we find the Holy Grail
Maybe the love will then prevail

-o-o-o-

~ Loosely in the Sky? ~

Vicar *(A Good Story… It's Gospel)*

What can the vicar teach us all
Except to heed the Church's call?
Clean living's next to God he'll say
A pristine chapel wins the day

His teachings are vicarious
God's will through him passed on to us
His sermon on a Sunday plied
Handed down from pulpit high

The scriptures which are writ in stone
May pare our morals to the bone
Preordained behaviour might
As He's decreed lead us to light

But if we take a closer look
There's lots beyond the old Good Book
Twixt Heaven and Earth more things there are
Than we would think when viewed afar

-o-o-o-

~ Pray Tell ~

Lamplighter *(A Light Cycle)* *

Dusk comes on, it'll soon be dark
The dogs a-clamouring do bark
Lurking in the gathering fog
Strays abroad, those London dogs

Down close by the dockside yards
The lamplighter is working hard
Pole is lifted, taper glowing
Gas ignites, long shadows throwing

Courteous, righteous and nefarious
All these souls, both same and various
Scuttling home in helping light
Shaking off the fearful night

The nightmares soon from dawn will run
He's lamp-extinguisher become

-o-o-o-

~ On Your Wick ~

Florist *(Valentine's Day Masochist)*

Blue are violets, red are roses
A rhyming puzzle this sure posies
Especially on this special day
It's difficult in every way

Violet are blues and rose are reds
At least the ones in my raised beds
So if you must some colours pick
To all true tints be sure to stick

Now red is primary so is blue
Other colours are mixed hue
Except for yellow also prime
I'm really struggling with these rhymes

So ditch the violet and the rose
Work on scent and trust your nose
For every colour's Heaven scent
Choose other flowers and be a gent

-o-o-o-

~ Petal Be the Day ~

14

Porter *(Have a Drink on Me)*

Uniformed upon the station
The porter carries all the nation
Suitcases and portmanteaux
Pigeons cooing, cocks that crow

The hustle, and the bustle too
Absorbing it with work to do
His old sack barrow close at hand
Using it when weight demands

In the dark depths of the night
Moving luggage making light
This human trolley serving crowds
Sherpa Tenzing would be proud

But now he's old, his back is bent
Fallen arches, muscles spent
He needs a stick to walk, and how
A porter would be welcome now

-o-o-o-

~ Handlers' Messiah ~

Ballet Dancer *(Sore Points)* *

When young she yearned for ballet dancing
On the stage such dandy prancing
The ballet school loomed large for her
Once enrolled she'd naught but purr

She learned the moves there is no doubt
Elancer she would dart about
And g*lisser* gliding to and fro
Relever she soon rose you know

But then *etendre* patience stretched
At *plier* bending she just wretched
So turning *tourner* she gave in
Jumped off *sauter* on a whim

After all was done and said
She took up breakdancing instead

-o-o-o-

~ Gone Lake ~

Actor *(Stage Left)*

Now Shakespeare was a shrewd old dude
His plays were sometimes outright rude
And actors down through age on age
Have played the naughties on the stage

His Winter's Tale's of late re-fledged
With nude scenes now incorporated
The players are quite rightly shocked
Some of the parts are now half-cocked

This new interpretation brash
The female lead thought it all trash
She was having none of this
'This new script surely takes the piss'

She went stage left and left the stage
Exits pursued by bare... outraged
Against the script she fiercely railed
For out had popped a winter's tail

-o-o-o-

~ Chick in Wings ~

Fletcher *(Kill or be Quilled)* *

Archers all admired his skill
At feathering arrows he was brill
Straight as a die those darts did fly
They even caught King Harold's eye

The Bayeux 'broidery shows quite plain
In the blink of an eye the king was slain
The bowmen then at Agincourt
Two fingers up, the French did taunt

'A feather in your cap my lad,'
Said William Tell, the young boy's dad
While Robin Hood I'll have you know
Did Marion woo with arrow and bow

Yet fletcher's story stays untold
Sparse mention of his crucial role

-o-o-o-

~ Flight Hipping ~

Site Foreman *(Cuts Enthuses)* *

When but a lad of ten and three
A building site was the place to be
In holidays I'd meet my friends
With piles of bricks we'd make our dens

We'd joust with heavy scaffold poles
And stand on nails, shoes sprouting holes
We'd footle in cement-stained mud
Boasting hankies stained with blood

I got a job on leaving school
Progressed from time upon the tools
A foreman I became quite quick
To safety rules I now must stick

If only I could just retrain
So I could joust all day again

-o-o-o-

~ Mortar This ~

Solicitor *(Newsagent Provocateur)* *

'I want a lawyer!' he insisted
'These levelled charges are so twisted
I went in just to buy a paper
Got embroiled in that there caper'

'The man said "Hold this just a sec"
While his wallet he did check
Police arrived and off he panted
On me the weapon he had planted'

'I'd never held a gun before
Until I went in through that door
It shook me up, I'm telling you
It's left me in a right old stew'

Solicitor arrived... good grief!
Turned out to be the would-be thief

-o-o-o-

~ Lawyer, Lawyer ~

Bus Conductor *(Ring my Bell)*

The number 99 was coming
Fred the ageing athlete running
He vowed to catch it come what may
The next was due the following day

The driver saw him sprinting fast
And thought he might just sail right past
Conductor Janet was more kind
She'd never leave a soul behind

And so our Janet rang the bell
The driver screeched the bus like Hell
And Fred came boarding breathlessly
But fainted on the platform see

So Janet gave the kiss of life
She presently became his wife
And so they ride the Discount Rover
They visit places now all over

-o-o-o-

~ Tickets Please, Don't They ~

House Builder *(Better Slate than Clever)* *

There was a bright young architect
Whose vision spelled out mere effect
Blinkered, he plumped for aesthetics
What went before deemed so pathetic

The three little pigs gave out a groan
'Straw won't build a kingly home!
Why ditch the bricks and mortar mate?
 Don't rely on sticky tape'

The builder too was none too sure
'Change to something more secure
Use steel lintels, ditch the plastic
Don't rely on glue and mastic'

The house now won't crash round folks' ears
It'll not fall down in a thousand years

-o-o-o-

~ Artificial Construct? ~

22

Musician *(Devil Clef)* *

I've learned to play the clarinet
From that there YouTube on the Net
I'll soon become a true celeb
Thanks to the dear old World Wide Web

With mallets for my xylophone
I make a plinky plonky tone
Ambira? Sistrum? What are they?
I acquired them along the way

My guitars, twelve-string, lead and base
Every instrument I'll face
Without a doubt I have them all
'Cacophony!' I hear you call

As multi-instrumentalist
I'll drive you slowly round the twist

-o-o-o-

~ Sound Proposition ~

Dentist *(Tooth be Told)*

'Open wide,' she says to him
'With needle and drill, I'm going in
I'll tackle that deep cavity
So grit your teeth, we'll be done by tea'

The poor bloke winces, closes eyes
Deep in the chair he's petrified
She drills and drills for ever more
He's sure she's dug through to his jaw

She then assures 'I won't be long'
He can't now feel his swelling tongue
Then leaning closer in she cries
And disappears deep down inside

The nurse she grabs her by the feet
Extracting her, the move is neat
The dentist straightens up her gown
And recommends she'll fit a crown

-o-o-o-

~ Molar Mauler ~

Palfreyman *(Soon My Prance Will Come)* *

Go ride a cock-horse to Banbury Cross
The ladies all love such a fine ambling hoss
They'll all want to ride one, definite sure
When saddled with journeys, since ages of yore

The Palfreyman caters with such a fair breed
Ensuring the ladies have desirable steeds
Expensive they may be, but so highly prized
She shall have palfreys wherever she rides

Rings and sweet bells on her fingers and toes?
A good horse provided, she'll not wish for those
The knights will compete for her favours withal
Her white horse, her palfrey fresh from the stall

But when all's completed, all said and done
Despite all the journeying, home is more fun

-o-o-o-

~ Heaven's Gait? ~

Jeweller *(Alfred's Gem)*

'*Aelfred Mec Heht Gewyrcan* did
For many years I laid full hid
King Alfred had me made, you know
Some eleven hundred years ago'

In southern England you will ken
Anglo-Saxon Wessex then
The years have passed, the pages read
Words all written, many said

A pointer stick it was at first
until it died and went to earth
Since then it's lost its handle on things
And yet survived long-suffering kings

It's seen off Vikings, Normans too
It's seen such sad things that men do
Another, brighter day will come
When all will see fair Albion

-o-o-o-

~ A Pointer in Case ~

Deep Sea Diver *(Isolation Thanks)* *

Precious are the coral reefs
Losing them would bring us grief
The myriads of shoaling fishes
Evoke our very dearest wishes

Silvered sunbeams shafting fall
Bathing all in warmth withal
But snorkels are for shallow wimps
A diving bell is best, methinks

I'm down in that bloke Jones's locker
People think I'm off my rocker
It's peaceful though, can't hear a sound
Except for whale song, so profound

The deep dark water solace brings
Timeless in the scheme of things

-o-o-o-

~ Fathom It ~

Lecturer *(Uni Versatile?)* *

He lectured down the local Poly
Teaching loads of useful knowledge
Brickies, plumbers, chippies too
Engineers, a solid crew

But now upmarket they did go
As Techs became a big no-no
A Uni now the old place is
And paying students to it whizz

It's media studies now you see
Or classics, or philosophy
But those skills our poor chap did lack
Next term they wouldn't have him back

Hard skills now a backseat take
Please bring them back for Heaven's sake

-o-o-o-

~ Tooled Up ~

28

Taxidermist *(The Stuff of Nightmares)*

A pachyderm you might well say
A taxidermist night and day
By nature he was so thick-skinned
His training he could not rescind

'I'll take the animals that died
So they can stay right by your side
Arsenic, mercury and benzene
All helping to preserve the genes'

Birds and mammals he'd attempt
Such specimens you'd never have dreamt
The sizes grew, they'd not relent
Rhino, hippo, elephant

His downfall was the great blue whale
The stuffing was beyond the pale
The real problem, the truth to tell
A glass dome was impossible

-o-o-o-

~ Heaven Preserve Us ~

Barista *(The Lore's the Law)*

Good coffee she wished to prepare
Where high-class shoppers did repair
'Sorry, miss we want a mister
To be our Resident Barista'

'How can you do this thing to me?
It's so discriminatory'
'Very well, but just a trial
A week for us to test your style'

Out she set and she did prove
Her serving style was in the groove
First customer defiant sat
'I want it white, I tell you flat'

'Arabica! You'll get it black
No sugar too, we won't have that
As for cups, we charge you see
And you can't have the caffeine free'

-o-o-o-

~ Where's Ya Bean? ~

Park Keeper *(The Great Migration)* *

When first a keeper she became
The outdoor life she'd entertained
But much these days is admin based
The paperwork she couldn't face

Ignoring it she went outside
She wanted fresh air to provide
She strolled the paths and skirted lakes
This was the dream she'd undertake

Her boss was all municipal
Complained that her in-tray was full
Her out-tray was the litter bin
She tipped it up all over him

She left and got a job abroad
The Serengeti her reward

-o-o-o-

~ Swings and Roustabouts ~

Neighbour *(A Sound Proposition)* *

My neighbour down at number three
I swore would be the death of me
He plays his music very loud
With massive speakers he's endowed

I asked him to turn down the noise
That all my very peace destroys
He said it's not the same played soft
So I decided I was off

I moved out to the country fast
A cottage with some quiet at last
But silence drove me quite insane
So I moved back to town again

And now I beg my neighbours dear
Turn up the sound so I can hear!

-o-o-o-

~ The Vinyl Straw ~

Civil Engineer *(Is He Barred?)*

He worshipped Brunel when a lad
When Meccano he'd first had
To build a bridge would give him joy
He'd dreamed of it since just a boy

With letters now after his name
He'd built a bridge for high-speed trains
The first one he jumped on with pride
He went along just for the ride

His calculations were adrift
The bridge collapsed, the piers did shift
The train it managed to speed clear
No lives were lost despite his fears

The Institution banned him fast
That bridge had proved to be his last
For want of several R.S.J.s
He now just with Meccano plays

-o-o-o-

~ Nuts and Blots ~

Hatter *(Who Wants to be a Milliner?)*

They'd asked 'Why make those hats you fool?'
Upon the day that he left school
'It'll be a feather in my cap'
He'd said to those depressive chaps

So skilful hatter he became
No one better at the game
But carroting with Mercury
Sent him batty don't you see

Though brimming with self-confidence
His conversations made no sense
To the asylum he was led
An Alice band playing in his head

If only he'd abandoned hats
To be a plumber instead perhaps
But then the lead would treat him bad
And send him there likewise... quite mad

-o-o-o-

~ Heading for a Fall ~

King *(Moan Arch)* *

Sitting on this throne all day
I feel they all should go away
The courtesans, the hangers-on
I wish they'd all be up and gone

My kingship's made me all remote
Perhaps I should allow a vote
For monarchy with the power it holds
Just brings me people harsh and cold

A President's the answer sure
Or P.M. that suits even more
That way, I'll have lots of friends
Who'll sympathetically attend

I shall replace my kingy thing
Democracy! the very thing

-o-o-o-

~ Divine Wrong? ~

Teacher *(She Was the Tops)*

Her pupils didn't see eye to eye
And so she gasped a desperate sigh
She'd always had a heart felt yearning
To bottom out this seat of learning

And so vast reams of homework set
'I'll sort these rebels out'… and yet
The students thought her such a burk
So she was tied up in her work

'Let me loose,' she'd cried in vain
Embarrassment worse than the pain
Next morning homework was presented
And once untied she swift relented

She joined the circus with a frown
And lived her life with circus clowns
The trapeze was her saving grace
It was by far the safer place

-o-o-o-

~ A Touch of Class ~

Photographer *(Negative Equity)*

Along the prom he plies his trade
It's where his frugal living's made
Algernon the camera man
Snaps tourists boldly when he can

'Come to the pier at half-past three
I'll be there with your prints you see'
But George and Elsie take offence
To privacy they give defence

They grab the camera like a flash
And to the railings make a dash
They chuck the Kodak in the sea
And go off for their posh cream tea

So poor old Algy is bereft
He can't believe they've upped and left
His master-plan is all undone
The camera's tide-borne on the run

-o-o-o-

~ Make It Snappy ~

Airman *(Winging It)* *

He flew into the vast blue sky
A distant spec in someone's eye
He'd headed up there on a whim
Across the azure Heavens to skim

But then the clouds came rolling in
Such little things didn't bother him
He climbed all altitudinous
At least three miles with ne'er a fuss

Soon all the cumulus dissolved
He spied the fields below unfold
And up there in the firmament
He saw how Earth's horizon's bent

A distant church's clock did chime
He from the simulator climbed

-o-o-o-

~ A Flight of Fancy ~

Cartoonist *(Picture This)*

His drawing skills he ever plies
Oft looking for the funny side
The daily news can all seem grim
He plays with it upon a whim

He'll sometimes scribble without pause
But then sophisticated draws
A gem of humour with a spark
Absurdity dispelling dark

He'll find light-heartedness in grief
And poke some fun at our beliefs
He'll make us laugh then make us cry
He'll break our hearts or split our sides

An erudite display of wit
Or sometimes his ideas are shit
But all in all if we ignore
We'll lose that twinkle ever more

-o-o-o-

~ Just a Strip Poker? ~

Composer *(A Man of Notes)* *

I'll start with Brahms, and Liszt a few
Vivaldi's, full of life its true
Bach to the future he did look
Behoved Beethoven tunes to cook

Tchaikovsky's obviously there
That Wagner had an Aryan air
Chopin chopped and changed his ways
While Mozart moped around all day

Strauss was stressed much of the time
Hayden had an awesome prime
Handel, bright you'll sure find it
Debussy, busy showed true grit

What every one of them did do
Is write their music just for you

-o-o-o-

~ Super-classical-ifragilisticexpialidocious ~

Playwright *(Play Wrong)*

He dreamed of putting on a play
'My writing skills are here to stay
A Comedy or tragedy
Combine the two, let plots run free'

But when he tried to make it work
His chosen funder went berserk
'It's not commercial don't you see?
No money there for you or me'

He hesitated now to write
Creative juices in a plight
He'd thought his words were all spot on
But funders' interest had all gone

Then he had a bright idea
He wrote again, dispelling fear
He parodied the stilted stage
And almost earned a living wage

-o-o-o-

~ Stage Fright ~

Mathematician *(It Just Didn't Add Up)*

After years of teaching kids
He felt he might go off the skids
The stress was costing him so dear
He sighed 'my number's up, I fear'

He could do naught but sit and scream
Insoluble, equations seemed
Not solving them by usual paths
He felt nonplussed by all the maths

His peers' opinions did divide
Retire he must, he would decide
Times were hard, respect was gone
Time to put his bike clips on

Once back home he was morose
Insanity was stalking close
And then soon on a sorry day
They took the poor old chap away

-o-o-o-

~ Summing It Up ~

Tree Surgeon *(Branch Office)* *

When canopies require a lift
Attention swift is in my gift
As if by magic skill somehow
I'll tend to trees, I'll take a bough

I'll tend a tree through many a year
So it lives on, new seasons clear
The dead wood I will cut away
All for the new growth to make way

While foxes bark and winter bites
And owls hoot haunting on dark nights
The buds are forming secretly
In spring they'll burst on every tree

New season comes and birds do sing
And trees will add another ring

-o-o-o-

~ A Trunk Calling ~

Footballer *(It's a Game of Strong Calves)*

Fifties football down the park
Sunday mornings, what a lark
Laundered shirts and dubbin'd boots
Mud for grass… oh, what a hoot

Shin pads made with rough bamboo
Corner flags on four by two
Studs of laminated leather
Rain or snow, no heed to weather

Fame and fortune I will seek
I'll earn at least five quid a week
I'll play for Spurs, I am no fool
Or Manchester, or Liverpool

And when my ageing bones all creak
And muscles too have gone all weak
I'll hang those boots up on a hook
Watch Premier League… what the f***

-o-o-o-

~ Get Out of Goal Free! ~

Bus Driver *(Open Top?)*

Jim pondered all the weekend through
What on earth was he to do?
You'd not believe the dreadful stress
His bus was now conductor-less

Unsettled thoughts were wandering free
As in a dream he seemed to be
He'd never handled money see
He couldn't count to take the fee

Turning out of Lupin Lane
Poor old Jim felt stressed again
Then once upon the open road
His mind forgot the heavy load

A railway bridge jumped out at him
A sudden obstacle for Jim
Forgetting it's a double-decker
He's branded now a big bus wrecker

-o-o-o-

~ Taking Route ~

Architect *(1660s Sick)*

The Great Plague came and it went
And was followed by a dreadful event
Poor London to The Fire submitted
Despite all endeavours committed

Foul fate was determined to intrude
King Charles's realm was sore bruised
But Wrenovation was close at hand
London City's resurrected so grand

With Saint Paul's Cathedral gone
And many churches, the list went on
Good Christopher Wren stood up proud
He rebuilt and it still speaks loud

O'er the world in similar plights
New architects will conquer night
London rebuilt's not alone
'Resurgam' elsewhere writ in stone

-o-o-o-

~ Foundation's Tone ~

Private Investigator *(Ricky Dicky)* *

When Rick retired and left the Force
He just got bored at home of course
And so he advertised his skills
'I'll research all your perceived ills'

Maud, pillar of society
Agreed with him a modest fee
She asked him to investigate
Her husband Dick oft out so late

The Private Dick, employed by Maud
Did soon find Rick to be a fraud
He'd got two other women hid
And Private Dick did lift the lid

The Private Dick caught private Dick
Divorce ensued then, double quick

-o-o-o-

~ *Eye Aye* ~

Geisha *(Arty Facts)* *

A geisha I, since times long past
Professional to the very last
Japan's old customs I'll unfold
With music, dance and art untold

At banquets I'll attend the guests
Communication of the best
I'll show them fine calligraphy
And offer ceremonial tea

Yet in old times before the Yen
The geisha were in fact all men
Taikomochi jesters they
But times move on or so they say

Traditions handed down they be
All shadows of our history

-o-o-o-

~ Orientation ~

Plumber *(Lead Astray)*

The plumber filled with deep dismay
His flashings were all lead astray
Two thieves had nicked them from his stash
And round the bend they both had dashed

He thought to give chase with great haste
But all his zeal just seemed misplaced
For despite the heavy loot
His desperate dash it bore no fruit

Until one thief, to spite his scheme
His pocket's seams were weak it seems
His wallet full of cash it fell
It held his home address as well

The plumber one night paid a call
And quietly he scaled a wall
Once on the roof he peeled the lead
And our dear thief got soaked in bed

-o-o-o-

~ Midnight Flasher ~

Crusader *(George's Flag Rant)* *

A Roman, Cappadocia born
I died in Lydda, all forlorn
I lay so quiet eight hundred years
Before folk did prick up their ears

Then they decided I'd crusaded
I'd slain a dragon quite unaided
A Patron Saint I fast became
For England, Moscow and for Spain

A football team my flag thinks fit
Skinheads too have hijacked it
My dying day's commemorated
Shakespeare's birth with it conflated

With plagiarists I am be-knighted
I wish I had been copyrighted

-o-o-o-

~ Saint's Preserve ~

Legal Secretary *(Dirty Deeds)* *

I'm well versed in conveyancing
My typewriter, I make it sing
Seventy words a minute plus
I turn out deeds without a fuss

My boss is down the Court today
While he's away this mouse will play
I'll type my own work here instead
Put this next chapter fast to bed

My murder plot is building nice
Solicitors will pay the price
Imperial 66 my muse
The murder weapon that I choose

And when I'm published hang it all
With the royalties I'll have a ball

-o-o-o-

~ Not My Type ~

Journalist *(Headline to Breadline)*

Important news was to be found
But Jim the journalist did frown
'I can't report this serious stuff
With trivia I'd be more chuffed'

Frivolous stories he preferred
And garnished them with every word
Hyperbole he did bestow
Terrier like he'd not let go

Until one day some news so dire
Upon the hack it did backfire
Redundancy swift fell on him
His pension plan went in the bin

And now he sits at home morose
Glued to TV news engrossed
The stories all invoke his own
And drive him bonkers sat alone

-o-o-o-

~ Slow News Is Good News? ~

Inventor *(Eureka!)*

Discovering something no-one knew
It pre-existed, certain true
Novel he contrived to make it
For copyright he even faked it

He claimed it as his own design
Though it had been there all the time
You can't deny when said and done
There's nothing new 'neath moon or sun

For man invents invention sure
He finds it hid and nothing more
Look in cupboards you will find
An earlier version, though unsigned

It may not be quite clearly marked
Stealthily it was just parked
Invention then is naught but myth
With treasures left for us as gifts

-o-o-o-

~ Known Unknowns ~

53

Morris Dancer *(Summoned by Beers)* *

Beguiled by the tinkling bells
Drifting on the breeze to tell
The much revered old folky-tales
Tradition so mysterious veiled

The music did intoxicate
Ribbons and hankies did conflate
Rag coats and clogs and sturdy sticks
With baldricks added to the mix

But when it all came down to land
With tankards tightly held in hand
All that mattered was good ale
The rest's significance did pale

Tradition only really thrived
When the Morris dancers' beer arrived

-o-o-o-

~ Arts and Craft Beers ~

Caretaker *(Old School)* *

He started work at half-past-six
Lit the boiler with chopped sticks
Shovelled coke up from the bay
'Can't have kids sit cold all day'

He'd clear the toilets when they blocked
Flushed with pride when tap leaks stopped
No one got the tradesmen in
They knew they could rely on him

They retired him at sixty-five
His pension just kept him alive
At home his youth he did recall
They'd had no caretaker at all

For all those years in old brown smocks
They'd bought him one o' them there clocks

-o-o-o-

~ A Stack of All Trades ~

Traffic Warden *(Bay Watch)*

Just the ticket that's his job
He only earns an honest bob
A benefactor, that's his role
As he along the streets patrols

'Just five minutes mate,' they say
As with the rules they try to play
So he decides who stays or goes
The sods they keep him on his toes

Some from streets they should be banned
While some just need a helping hand
He gives the worthy ones some time
While others he decides to fine

And when the long day's been and gone
His wife pours him a drink quite strong
'Don't park your feet on that there couch'
She clips his ear and he cries 'Ouch!'

-o-o-o-

~ Park Life ~

Queen *(April Flowers) ***

With generations on the run
I knew one day the call would come
And through these ever-fleeting years
Like you, I've had my hopes and fears

Though sometimes people haven't cared
Such joyous times I've often shared
We all will have our precious times
The memories resilient chime

Companionship is dear to all
It's been that way since 'fore the Fall
Now all I ask is peace and calm
For people not to come to harm

And now I've reached my ninety-sixth
I have hopes on the future fixed

-o-o-o-

~ Crowning Story ~

D.J. *(The Jox Pop)* *

My decks are best, I tell you all
The halls and clubs do nightly call
And bows I'll take occasionally
It's holy entertainment see

My vinyl discs include some gems
Well worth scratching now and then
With volume and the bass up full
My evenings are just never dull

I'll cater for all tastes you know
Dubstep, Garage, House and so
My reverb employs latest tech
My pint glass just now hit the deck

I'll dance you to a standstill yet
And hit you with a second set

-o-o-o-

~ Slick Disc ~

Baker *(A Grain of Struth)*

The old street that's called Pudding Lane
They say is where that fire was lain
It was a grate fire, that is true
French baker bidding all adieu

The Mayor might just take the piss
Of women to put right all this
But bucketfuls just wouldn't work
What a really stupid berk

Samuel Pepys, close to the fire
He witnessed devastation dire
The Navy Clerk got digging fast
So his Parmesan might last

He dug until the morning came
Not thinking there among the flames
If he'd included bread to roast
He'd invent hot cheese on toast

-o-o-o-

~ Rising to the Occasion ~

Lock Keeper *(Home from Roam)* *

The old canal was his own home
He'd no desire far to roam
The idyll of the waters calm
The cottage too was full of charm

The lock keeper, old Arthur Flynn
Would see the painted boats glide in
Bargees, smiles upon their faces
Majestic horses in the traces

He worked the sluices up then down
He'd see to it with nary a frown
And when the sun went down at night
With boats moored up and doors shut tight…

In candle light he'd take a beer
'There ain't no troubles come round here'

-o-o-o-

~ Inland Water Praise ~

Yoga Instructor *(An Invite to Supple)* *

Upon his yoga mat he sat
Akin to the proverbial cat
His mentor also she did sit
He thought of her as rather fit

He followed her instructions close
Defeated though, he felt morose
Like plaited liquorice she contorting
Cramp in his legs, it needed sorting

He asked her out to supper though
She replied 'Where shall we go?'
'A nice Italian eating place'
But one dish he just couldn't face…

Spaghetti was right out of bounds
He couldn't face those writhing mounds

-o-o-o-

~ Relapsing Exercise ~

Bag Lady *(Trundle Bundle)* *

A bent old lady passes by
'That's old Nettie,' some folk sigh
She's someone's granny that's for sure
But no one knocks upon her door

Her old pram squeaks along all day
Full of junk all thrown away
Discarded by society
The junk that is, and poor Nettie

Wild hair and old clothes sad to see
The archetypal bag lady
Come cold rain, come blistering sun
Til dusk arrives her trek's not done

To think she once was in her prime
To come to this… a sad, sad time

-o-o-o-

~ Stepping Out ~

Historian *(Passed Times Pastime)*

Her father founded finding Pharaohs
Discovered villains and some heroes
All those years ago they were
Their lives now but a distant blur

Romans, Countrymen lent ears
Witness to the passing years
They'd opened up the world it seems
But soon to lose hold of their dreams

Hastening on she studied battles
Where conquered people lost their chattels
Saxon hordes left Saxon hoards
As Normans they did strut the boards

Horses, kingdoms came and went
To a car-park she was sent
She came across the Tudors too
Closer now to me and you

-o-o-o-

~ Past Prefect ~

63

Entrepreneur *(Bonne Chance)* *

I take between the rich and poor
I'm always knocking at the door
I'll buy and sell most anything
I can make a business sing

As middle man I am renowned
I pick up businesses that drowned
That always caused some grave concern
And turn them into going turns

For me with my attractive pitch
Things come and go without a glitch
I've made some money, safe and sound
On the world's mad merry-go-round

But if I'm taxed right to the core
I just won't take it any more

-o-o-o-

~ Between You and Me ~

M.P. *(Suffer Us Yet)* *

Elections they will come and go
So polling day's when you must show
I won't make you cross, you'll see
If you will mark your cross for me

Those schemes that feature in your dreams
They top my list, you'll have the cream
My programme's bound to float your boat
You can't go wrong, just give your vote

Arcadia is close at hand
I'm sure you want a peaceful land
The other lot just can't be right
Their policies would you benight

Oh dear, the exit polls aren't good
My slick campaign has been a dud

-o-o-o-

~ Let's Have a Party ~

Signalman *(Rail Stale)*

Efficiency was his watchword
To make mistakes would be absurd
He'd be there in his box by dawn
Early bed meant ne'er a yawn

But then one day he met a mate
She'd help him out until quite late
A single man he should have stayed
Efficiency began to fade

Half asleep while on the job
A warning bell he off did fob
He missed the points change that's a fact
The 12.15 went off the tracks

At least no passengers were killed
But sacking him was soon fulfilled
His wife she left him all undone
A signal woman she's become

-o-o-o-

~ All Steamed Up ~

Sales Executive *(Balance Heat)* *

Dave's salary is really measly
Paying bills for him ain't easy
But year-end figures out today
Should bring a bonus into play

He's sold the brand the whole year through
Red figures turning black and blue
The graphs are riding upwards now
He's turned performance round somehow

Yet the boss has other plans
On all the dosh he has his hands
His package is the biggest yet
While Dave won't even bonus get

The boss is now in A & E
No shrinking violet Dave you see

-o-o-o-

~ Steal the Deal ~

Dustman *(Bin and Gone)* *

Once I was a dustman called
Until my job was overhauled
I came to cart your crap away
Breathing dust and grime all day

A scavenger I might be called
This unjust name it did appal
Yet that old bike was worth a ride
It made a few bob on the side

'Waste Management,' that's now the game
'Disposal Technician,' I'm named
I wear thick gloves, and masks at times
Dealing with your weekly grime

Magpie, I am called no more
Respectable right to the core

-o-o-o-

~ Crossing the Rubbish-con ~

Pantomime Dame *(He, She)*

The Panto season's been and gone
And now the dress he will not don
Although he loves it on the stage
In life it's not for him the rage

This way of dressing makes some cross
He thinks to be a Panto hoss
'Neigh lad,' they told him so plain
'We want you in that dress again'

'Because we know it draws the crowds
They cheer for you exceeding loud
Leave the equine far behind
For it's affront to humour kind'

'On principal… a girl's the boy
Without it joy would surely cloy
Entertaining is our mission
Gender switching is tradition'

-o-o-o-

~ Oh, Yes It Is! ~

Pathologist *(On the Right Path)*

Pathologist? He is morose
He's studying paving stones up close
They're copiously stained with blood
Cadaver where a man once stood

The latex gloves they serve him well
But they don't take away the smell
He nonetheless must get to work
He's not inclined to stand and shirk

The body, so no one can see
Is taken to the mortuary
All foreign bodies cleared away
For him to work 'til close of day

His task it is now soon renewed
He gathers up his tools anew
He's no pathologist it's true…
A slab-layer with a job to do

-o-o-o-

~ Paths of Gory ~

Model Maker *(The Hobby Lobby) ***

Remember that Meccano set?
Best thing before sliced bread, and yet
When Air-fix models came along
With not much telly, couldn't go wrong

Spitfires, Stukas, were the craze
Then ships and cars and railways
Hornby Dublo, OO gauge
The track, the stations, all the rage

The old wood building blocks were gone
But later Lego came along
Entire cities, whole rooms filled
Vast modular design and build

Now digital's soon all there'll be
With VR, AR... reality?

-o-o-o-

~ Glue Spiffing ~

Brewer *(Mash Up)*

The vats were bubbling, what a scent
The best smell in the firmament
The yeast, the hops, the barley malt
The odours he did so exalt

Then disaster struck one day
The brewer's smell just went away
He felt he could make beer no more
His doctor couldn't find a cure

A specialist he did implore
His nasal passage to explore
She poked and prodded vigorously
So past his septum she could see

And after searching for some time
She saw the problem, how sublime
Plugs of yeast extracted then
The brewer set to work again

-o-o-o-

~ Keep a Clear Head ~

Sculptor *(Captured in Stone)*

Chipping at the block of stone
The sculptor works all on his own
Carefully he clips and chips
Forming noses, eyes and lips

Working like a man possessed
Until the soft clean stone is dressed
Until it's set free like a bird
Speaking louder than all words

The human form is rendered true
Then late at night when dark ensues
Although the statue's stood enthralled
It springs to life and scales the walls

They see the statue's upped and gone
And find it on the highway long
Chasing quarry, quarried stone
They bring it barbarous back home

-o-o-o-

~ Stoned Again? ~

Dancer *(Taking Steps)*

She tried all kinds of dance it's true
From Ballet class to Ballroom too
Quickstep, Foxtrot, Waltz and Smooth
Learning dancing, in the groove

Samba, Rumba, Boogaloo
Tango was erotic too
Merengue, Cha Cha and the Jive
'Twas so good to be alive

Salsa rhythms so divine
While Line Dancing kept her in line
Whirling Sufi ecstasies
Cutting all the shapes that pleased

But in the end she chose the Morris
Went along with her friend Doris
The men were quite put out, it seems
The women were the best they'd seen

-o-o-o-

~ Partners in Time ~

Choreographer *(Step On It)* *

I'll teach you how to dance with feeling
Have you dancing on the ceiling
High kicks, lifts, are my trademarks
I'm good at this here dancing lark

Whichever rhythm you may choose
I'll give you magic dancing shoes
You'll find so vigorous my routines
You could well split those tight blue jeans

Whatever music floats your boat
Upon the music you will float
Your fans will swoon, I do believe
Ovations wild you will receive

I guarantee within a year
You'll have a thriving dance career

-o-o-o-

~ Top of the Hops ~

Horse Whisperer *(Tails from the Shires)* *

I'm apt to whisper to my horse
He whispers back to me of course
He tells me precious tales you see
Passed down from his proud family

His stories come from those before
They tell of life on dales and moors
When ancestors had pulled the plough
Or worked the pits with sweating brow

Some had worked on the canals
Roped to narrow boats and all
Transporting coal before trains came
Treading on through wind and rain

Rewarding him with hay and oats
I quietly share his anecdotes

-o-o-o-

~ In the Hear and Plough ~

Investment Manager *(Buy and Buy)*

'I know where the money is
I'm so well versed in this here biz
Stocks and shares are my best friends
Though there value just depends'

'I can make the numbers dance
Your vast portfolio to enhance
Paltry ventures I will shun
And eggs in baskets? I'll have none'

And so he did for Corporates gamble
As if upon a country ramble
Buying here and selling there
Sometime Bull and sometimes Bear

Then one day it all went wrong
Investments going for a song
He realised that he'd been had
His tulip bulbs had all gone bad

-o-o-o-

~ Trade Raid ~

Etymologist *(Wordy Opponent)* *

She's in her favourite library
At Cambridge University
Searching through old texts and things
Looking for lost origins

Bob walks in, all airs and graces
Determined he'll find older traces
He spouts abrupt, curmudgeonly
That he'll delve back further than she

She hasn't reckoned on meeting Bob
And wishes he would shut his gob
He just goes on and on… and on
She bites her lip, then patience gone…

'Look, kind sir, you are a tw**
Go find the origin of that'

-o-o-o-

~ Word for Words ~

Painter & Decorator *(Lick Her Paint?)* *

Her C.V. say it all it seems
She'll decorate to match your dreams
The subtle shades of soft sage greens
Calm cadences of clotted creams

She'll spend for you a bob or two
Using Dulux in the loo
But if you really want it all
She'll paint the rest with Farrow and Ball

And when it comes to papering
The size of it will make you sing
On walls, the pattern drop's just right
Her ceilings really reach the heights

The Queen will decorate her yet
A new year's honour's a safe bet

-o-o-o-

~ A Brush with the Lore ~

Ticket Inspector *(Getting into Characters)* *

The ticket man calls 'tickets please!'
Glides the corridors with ease
The six-fifteen from Waterloo
Is transporting a motley crew

Sweeney Todd can't find his ticket
Complains that Mrs Lovett's nicked it
The inspector with his trusty clipper
Is sure he's just seen Jack the Ripper

What the Dickens is going on?
Rochester station's been and gone
Estella's with Miss Havisham
While Fagin's off to Faversham

Oliver's hungry, just a tad
And Sykes's Bullseye's barking mad

-o-o-o-

~ A Clip Round the Years ~

Statistician *(Pi in the Sky)*

Her spreadsheets were all works of art
The media hooked right from the start
Believing every word she said
Stats revered with greatest dread

Adopting all, they'd not decry
Her charts and circles, pie and pi
Afforded truth with Gantt regard
But soon hoist by their own petard

Their ratings fell eventually
The public through them they did see
Full facts they wanted given straight
All potted info did berate

So now the statistician's gone
Venn charts sternly frowned upon
Bubble charts and bar charts too
Redundant without much ado

-o-o-o-

~ Your Number's Up ~

Geologist *(Stoned Again)*

She looks for rocks and all that biz
She's down-to-earth if anyone is
Ferreting in the marl and clay
Footling in the soil all day

She thought of throwing in the towel
Fed up scraping with her trowel
But then again she did take stock…
She'd stumbled on a bright green rock

Carbon dating proved of use
The Periodic Tables too
Ultrasound and sonic blast
Until she got results at last

'Diamonds? No thanks, can't you see
And rubies red are not for me
Fate's proved for me that in the end
Emeralds are a girl's best friend'

-o-o-o-

~ Get Your Rocks Off ~

Philatelist *(Stamp It Out)*

When she'd declared to friends at school
'I'm collecting stamps, they're really cool'
They'd said of her odd chosen craft
'It's only boys that are so daft'

But with her hobby she still stuck
Until she'd filled up all the book
She bought another album blank
Her collection soon with experts ranked

With sticking stamps she stuck for years
Teased right cruelly by her peers
The albums they just multiplied
She stacked them carefully with pride

Then one day having felt irate
She got her own back on her mates
A book fell from a towering stack
And there out popped a Penny Black

-o-o-o-

~ Funky Gibbons ~

Weaver *(Left Be-weft)* *

The South of France I miss it so
Sad forced to roam, a Huguenot
In Spitalfields I am of late
Set here in sixteen eighty-eight

My trade is weaving silk dear friend
And on the loom my time I spend
I'm wrapped up so in warp and weft
Of happiness I am bereft

Through Canterbury I came here
In London now these past two years
The English soon will build such mills
And hijack all our hard-won skills

Though English folk for silk do call
The weaver's life means bugger all

-o-o-o-

~ Disaster Looms ~

Policeman *(Banged to Rights)*

They said that he should pound the beat
Because he had enormous feet
He'd plod all day and plod all night
And give the burglars such a fright

A natural peeler with his eyes
He'd catch the crim'nals by surprise
Always ready with his truncheon
Even when sat down to luncheon

He'd apprehend them off the cuff
The smooth operators and the rough
The slippery characters he would pick
And cart them all off down the nick

The only trouble with all this
The sergeant said he was remiss
He was so keen, because of him
The cells were filled up to the brim

-o-o-o-

~ Bobby Dazzler! ~

85

Acrobat *(Flight of Fancy)*

The circus was in town again
The clowns were all so gleeful then
They hated being on the road
Their car was always being towed

Now acrobats enjoy the travelling
Rejoice to see the tents unravelling
Once on high on his trapeze
Jim had fallen for Louise

She picked him up when he went flying
Sawdust saving him from dying
He courted her up in the clouds
While playing to adoring crowds

He fancied her, she fancied him
They married soon upon a whim
He never ever let her slip
At last in life he'd got a grip

-o-o-o-

~ They're the Tops ~

Tramp *(Stepping Out in Time)* *

When I was young, the world out there
I tramped with purpose everywhere
From town to hamlet rain or shine
A world of oysters they were mine

The milestones came, the milestone went
Park benches were all free of rent
It was in truth the life I chose
High borne thoughts and well-worn clothes

My gabardine despite hot days
My holey boots brought carefree ways
Highways, byways travelling
An open road the very thing

But now with stiffness in my feet
I tramp no more, sat in the street

-o-o-o-

~ Miles Tones ~

News Presenter *(North, East, West, South)*

I'll give you all the daily news
Brought in by our camera crews
The wars across the planet rage
The same old tales on every page

The world is warming, that we know
Not just the climate, overtly so
The world seems busy beating drums
The autocue relays what comes

It sometimes seems unending farce
Will the world go up its arse?
Stoical, I try to be
I hide my thoughts from what you see

When I get home I wear a frown
And drink a shot of whisky down
There'll be a bright day I'm so sure
When strife we won't need to endure

-o-o-o-

~ Investi-Gate? ~

Magician *(It's in the Hands of Time)*

Top hat handy, cloak as well
He likes a rabbit truth to tell
Chatting with his Circle close
Lest he starts to feel morose

His sleight of hand can't be surpassed
He never seems to be outclassed
Yet into doldrums he does sink
Most always sad what e'er you think

Adroit his left hand, we can tell
His right hand dextrous is as well
For left seems right while right seems left
Yet still of laughter he's bereft

He'll smash your watch in his silk bag
While thinking still that life's a drag
Yet when the watch proves whole again
Gloom vanishes like summer rain

-o-o-o-

~ It's in the Hands of Time ~

Make-up Artist *(Let's Face It)* *

You couldn't see his face for paint
She'd made him look just what he ain't
Without the make-up he would fade
Obscure and wan upon the stage

The audience could see him now
He oft wished it not so some how
For when he corpsed or lost his words
Obscurity he much preferred

He got to like the glamourous look
And kept it when the bus he took
Such keen interest this provokes
He's propositioned by a bloke

From then a clean face he ensured
Except when he would strut the boards

-o-o-o-

~ Transported ~

Hermit *(Drift Would)* *

Around the grounds of stately homes
A hermit they'd employ to roam
Reclusive he would drift the grounds
At times he would the guests astound

In summer he wore little else
Than sandals, loincloth and a belt
In winter he would don a cloak
His hood would mystery invoke

His Panpipes lilting through the trees
Etherial upon the breeze
For hoity-toity girls and blokes
It Greek mythology evoked

Then on his weekly day of rest
He's down the pub for a pint of Best

-o-o-o-

~ Pandomestic ~

Fireman *(Bill's Drill)*

The sky lit up all bright as bright
Alarm bells ringing out that night
So down the pole they all did slide
And set out on their frantic ride

The engine swift, their feet were fleet
The crowds were gathering in the street
The house was burning so intense
Fireman Bill he jumped a fence

Lives in the balance they were hung
As Bill stepped on a ladder rung
He climbed up to the window high
And brought them each down by and by

So all was well as it turned out
He'd saved the day there is no doubt
On Bill it's said there's not a patch
Where fire's concerned there is no match

-o-o-o-

~ Hot Stuff ~

Forester *(He Would for the Trees)*

Trees to his mill were naught but grist
'Ere he became arboriculturist
The trees they'd hit the forest floor
Creating clearings evermore

But now he nurtures nature keen
And deems deforesting obscene
Ever growing fresh new species
Giving them allotted spaces

Even on the roads themselves he plants
Though motorists they rave and rant
Deciduous they shed their graces
Trunk roads now don't go to places

They fume and smoulder at his zeal
They can't believe that he's for real
'He's barking mad,' they cry as one
'It's obvious his logic's gone'

-o-o-o-

~ Embarkation ~

Chandler *(Alighting on Sorrows)* *

A farthing-dip tallow reed they can have cheap
But moulded wax candles will cost them deep
I'll light their way briefly to win or to lose
The chandlery stinks which ever they choose

I'll make a brief candle to serve them with light
To help them see dimly on a cold dark night
But soon comes a candle to light them to bed
That's what the nursery rhyme grimly has said

Down in grim Newgate his head they chop off
To bells of Old Bailey his cap he can't doff
St Sepulchre's surely will look on him grave
Too late for the wretch now his soul for to save

Yet chandeliers burn bright in rich men's homes
The candles aid them to write doleful tomes

-o-o-o-

~ Wicked ~

Miller *(He's Got the Wind Up)*

The wind it windeth every day
The miller's grain's not here to stay
The grist is put to endless use
The flour he makes is living proof

His windmill turns all through the night
Vast profits he has in his sights
As time goes by he bags it well
In hessian sacks, the lot to sell

He doesn't give the Church its tithe
And off with all the lot he drives
A load too heavy breaks a wheel
In anguish oh how he does squeal

The wind then blows with vicious strength
And sends him toppling all his length
He's gathered up sharply where he lay
Along with his avarice he's whisked away

-o-o-o-

~ What a Grind ~

Paperboy *(Print Stint)* *

I'd just turned twelve, back in the day
Had a tiring paper-round, down our way
Ten-bob a week for all that slog
No wonder people now read blogs

A hundred *Mercury's* was the deal
In need of that god's wingéd heels
Especial on a Thursday late
When 'classifieds' just added weight

Walking streets for all those hours
In summer heat and springtime showers
In winter frosts and autumn fogs
The mad blokes and their barking dogs

But when 'twas Christmas time again
The tips could bring in three-pound-ten

-o-o-o-

~ Symbiosis? ~

Newsagent *(Print Sprint) ***

He'd just turned thirteen, so he said
His paper-round was easy bread
Ten-bob a week for little work
Why do lads from such tasks shirk

Eighty *Mercury's* was the deal
A fair amount that should appeal
Especially on a Saturday night
When news was thin and papers light

Walking streets, idyllic hours
In summer sun and springtime flowers
In winter crisp and autumn mellow
The nice dogs owned by friendly fellows

Then when 'twas Christmas time again
The tips could bring in six-pound-ten

-o-o-o-

~ Symbiosis? ~

97

Motorbiker *(Leather Stray)* *

I love the sound when tyres squeal
I take sharp corners on two wheels
And if I drove a motor car
I'd do the same, it's best by far

My helmet sporting flames is sleek
My leathers are all flash, so chic
My pillion riders all feel faint
Considerate biker, that I ain't

I kick through all the gears at speed
I'm like an angry wasp indeed
With exhaust baffles all removed
The decibels are much improved

I've pushed the bike right to its limit
And now the engine's buggered, innit

-o-o-o-

~ Flashy Gears ~

Train Driver *(Just a Little Steam)*

When he grew up he wished to be
And engine driver fast and free
All steamed up and sparks a-flying
Travel at speed? No need of trying

So down the tracks his engine roared
The demon driver didn't pause
Raging through the station fast
As if that day it was his last

They'd buffed the engine's paintwork up
He hit the buffers, what bad luck
His engine died a death right there
But all escaped, no harm to hair

They kicked him out upon his ear
At last in life his station clear
'I'll work for Frankie's Dublo
By far a safer place to go'

-o-o-o-

~ Station Hairy! ~

Gondolier *(Venice from Heaven)* *

I ply the booming tourist trade
With gondola I've got it made
The punters love me through and through
Though punting's for the Cambridge crew

Now quanting is for Norfolk Broads
Don't you know, it all accords
Tread front to back the method used
With punting not to be confused

Legging's for those canal tunnels
On your back up to the gunwales
But if on rivers you would float
Rollocks are for rowing boats

What is all this hard work for?
Myself, I'll stick to the gondal oar

-o-o-o-

~ Canal Knowledge ~

Prime Minister *(Hear Hear, There There?)*

He's just cleared out his Cabinet
The bottles and the glasses, yet
He just can't make a true clean sweep
I guess it must be hard to sleep

The media won't let him be
Dismissing pressing things you see
Life's a gas for most of us
And climate change? Don't make a fuss

Now nuclear fusion's on the way
It'll solve our problems one fine day
But power's split, forces react
While party opposites detract

Determined though to Carrie on
Until all criticism's gone
When Westminster is full refurbed
We'll all be shaken if not stirred

-o-o-o-

~ Nr.10's Not a Prime Number, Unlike Nr.11 ~

Cleaner *(Sucking Up to the Boss)* *

'Are you the cleaner?' Harry asked
'Then if you are, get cracking fast
I can't abide one speck of dust
Use the vacuum if you must'

'With poor cleaning we've been blessed
This office always is a mess
It could be cleaner, I'm quite sure
Especially that there dusty floor'

And so she got the Hoover out
The carpet got a thorough bout
'It's not that clean,' flash Harry said
'Best start again dear, I'm afraid'

She turned the vacuum on to turbo
The staff all pondered 'Where did he go?'

-o-o-o-

~ Brush Off ~

Valet *(A Man in Vests?)*

Now Figgins he lived all alone
Not far from a stately home
A valet he once used to be
So applied for the job vacancy

'We've just filled the post before you
But a butler is needed now too
Do you think you could supervise others?
Regard them as sisters and brothers?'

'I suppose it would do for while
But wardrobes are more my style
I could give pressing clothes a rest
But a man I would dress to impress'

'For clothes maketh man I declare
I can dress a man quite debonair
A waistcoat (a 'vest') is the best
Appearance is all, I'd suggest'

-o-o-o-

~ Dresser Confessor ~

Stand-up Comedian *(Royal Flushed)* *

I've jested for the King you know
His favoured quips they forth did flow
I'd stand and prance whenever called
But if I failed he'd be appalled

My hat was quartered, red and yellow
And bells made me a merry fellow
All the Court I had in stitches
Was destined to enjoy such riches

Then one day I fell off a stool
Of course I did feel such a fool
My jester's stick impaled a leg
He kicked me out, just left to beg

Now I frequent the streets in town
And sadly quip while sitting down

-o-o-o-

~ *Sat Ire* ~

Tailor *(Ruff, Just This)*

He learned his trade from family
Was made to measure endlessly
With pantaloons and waistcoats too
The ruffs, the cuffs and more to do

His father and his uncle both
Were stocked to rafters with old cloth
Their shop, where fops and gents did go
Was opened many moons ago

His ancient forebears all were tailors
Their patronage included sailors
And army men regaled in braid
Traditional was all their trade

But now the clientele has changed
The fashions now seem so deranged
And even tee-shirts made to measure
Bring customers such fervent pleasure

-o-o-o-

~ What a Turn-up ~

Ambulance Driver *(Nine Nine - Fine)*

The bells are ringing loud and shrill
The sirens blaring, pass we will
The snow is falling, the wind forms drifts
Yet we shall all the patients shift

With monitors and drips employed
We launch ourselves into the void
God knows if we'll make it through
Despite the odds, we usually do

The night is dark, though short the way
The rush-hour seems to last all day
All do their best to clear a path
A & E in sight at last

Finally we face a hitch
So many vying for a pitch
Though the journey's screwed up heads
We'll keep folks warm in the queue for beds

-o-o-o-

~ Emerging, See ~

Illusionist *(All Boxed In)*

He sought to see his sister sawn
In half-a-tick an act was born
He built a box without a care
And placed poor Daphne straight in there

His D.I.Y. was not so good
Especially when he sawed some wood
And now this body of new work
Proves him even more a jerk

Measure twice and then cut once
Despite this mantra he's a dunce
Our Daphne now with blood stained vest
Was sure a cut above the rest

So with this act of wanton slicing
He with Daphne's life was dicing
And now he bows his head right down
For she stands closer to the ground

-o-o-o-

~ Two Part Act ~

Breakdown Engineer *(Tricky to Ride)* *

Down the lanes all bright and breezy
Driving carefree, life so easy
Un- then just become all -fettered
Spark-plug failed? Dud carburettor?

Call the breakdown service quick
Getting cold now, feeling sick
Carefree ride has turned all sour
Hope they come within the hour

Soon the bonnet is high-lifted
These engineers, they seem so gifted
He thought to use some special kit
And ferreted around a bit…

'Found your fault, no need of tools
Fuel tank's empty'… What a fool!

-o-o-o-

~ AA'd Venture ~

Petrol Pump Attendant *(30 Smiles/Gallon)*

Before redundant I was made
I relied upon the motor trade
The whiff of benzine in the air
High octane journeys here and there

The innocence of leaded fuel
Fossil fuels they were so cool
Gay ventures then, considered fair
Sun roof open, wind in hair

But now there's mounting pangs of guilt
Assault and battery factories built
Soon the cars will drive themselves
With Highway Codes left on the shelves

The Sat Nav telling us the way
I guess the planet still will pay
And then we'll all stay in our homes
The self-drive cars left free to roam

-o-o-o-

~ Driving Reign ~

Woodworker *(A Date With Carbon)* *

He works the wood it's plane to see
Against the grain it cannot be
Fraxinus and Fagus fair
He'll make a table or a chair

He's even fond of making stools
Though Quercus is unkind to tools
Carpinus is a favourite
While Ilex too is more than fit

Betula oft fits the bill
And Tilia is better still
Sorbus aucuparia
Spoiled for choice we surely are

Replenish them by planting more
And we could ask for nothing more

-o-o-o-

~ By Your Leaf ~

Film Director *(Personal Cut)*

I really must convey this story
All the nice bits and the gory
It seems the public like it scary
With cliff-hangers both tense and hairy

I'll get the close-ups carefully framed
I'll leave the actors feeling drained
With all the re-takes infinite
Cameras running half the night

If only life were just like this
Perfect murder, perfect kiss
The knotted rope, the twisted plot
I'll give the public all I've got

And when we've overdubbed the sound
And got our feet back on the ground
The tills will all ring merrily
There'll be a fortune there for me

-o-o-o-

~ In the Frame ~

Travel Agent *(Up Up and a Stay)*

Where would you like to go? I ask
Your pleasure's my allotted task
There's India and Thailand too
The whole wide world's awaiting you

Venice? Such a lovely place
The Caribbean's rather ace
Norway, Iceland, gay Peru
All with lots of things to do

I could arrange the South of France
Here's our brochure, take a glance
The Seychelles could just fit your bill
Especially if you've time to kill

'I'm thinking more of Skeggy, right
Blackpool's nice, I love the lights
I know you may think me right bland
But I love dear old Eng-a-land'

-o-o-o-

~ National Leisure ~

Telephone Receptionist *(It's a Calling)* *

'How may I help you?' I will ask
No irritation with dumb tasks
To everyone I'm so polite
I'm courteous, the very height

I keep my head, I'm never brusque
Amenable from dawn to dusk
Despite obnoxious callers too
I bite my lip, I tell you true

You'll never hear me moan or groan
When I'm on the telephone
If people are irate with me
I'll show respect wholeheartedly

Except just once… some awful toff
I told him he could bugger off

-o-o-o-

~ Don't Answer That ~

Lorry Driver *(Tyred of Waiting)*

He is the knight that rides our roads
Delivering the precious loads
We praise him for his efforts true
Unless behind him in a queue

And then it's his unfailing fault
'What is he doing? Stupid dolt!
He should be on the Motorway
Or trains should take his truck away'

Down the country roads we'll scoot
Forgiving farmers… if on foot
With cattle crossing and with sheep
Our terminus for a while can keep

But if a lorry's then involved
It rankles wild our very soul
In truth *in* traffic we are not
We *are* the traffic that we've got

-o-o-o-

~ Wheel Meet Again ~

Software Developer *(Security Upfront)* *

Inquiring since she first could speak
Such information she did seek
Technology her one true passion
And at her school it was the fashion

So she was destined for IT
But then they named it ICT
Communication new to her
Her chosen path became a blur

Developing software she's stopped
For soft *wear* she just thinks the tops
She's now designing bras it's true
IT supports, it's what she'll do

This new initiative she trusts
She will succeed by going bust

-o-o-o-

~ A Bit of a Hold-up ~

Welder *(Come Together)*

It never was coincidence
The welder's arc of influence
It gave him access to a club
No metalworker known would snub

When they met to have a pint
The welders, tanked up, drank all night
The riveters all went a hammering
Steam guns taken all to stammering

Between them all they built a ship
A big bridge too, then one did quip
'If we can work all day and night
Brunel's Kingdom comes out right'

So on their mettle they performed
Industrial Revolution dawned
Era there, where e'er you gaped
A vast ironic Empire shaped

-o-o-o-

~ A Joint Effort ~

Taxi Driver *(Fare's Fair)*

'Where to mate?' he asked his fare
'Wherever it is I'll take you there
I know The Knowledge back-of-hand
The routes all in my head are planned'

He wanted somewhere quite obscure
The driver hadn't heard before
Our hero cabbie was quite flummoxed
He felt right sick unto his stomach

A sweat broke out upon his brow
His head was set to spinning now
'I'm sorry guv, can't take you there
It's new to me I do declare'

'Then go to Hell,' the fare replied
The driver, well he nearly died
'I know where that is… been before'
He set off there and locked the doors

-o-o-o-

~ The Clock Is Running ~

117

Dart Player *(Stiff Opposition)* *

'I want to see three in a bed'
The captain of the darts team said
But William hit the wire, it's true
They lost the match and beer leg too

'Now look my lad,' said captain Keith
'That miss you made's beyond belief
We rely on you, you are the best
You always get three in a nest'

So when the return match was played
Bill's nerves had never been so frayed
Standing there upon the oche
He shook until his knees went knocky

But spot on were his darts, so strong
With Willy up they couldn't go wrong

-o-o-o-

~ Bull's High ~

118

Maid *(Pinny Afore)* *

A mother was in service when
A war had taken all the men
She skivvied for the upper classes
Making beds and washing glasses

She found respect to some degree
Though down below the stairs she be
Her husband, he was on the Somme
For four long years he had been gone

Yet he was luckier than most
He returned, they stood to toast
'To brighter days ahead for all
A war to end all wars withal'

But '39 she lived to rue
Her daughter a domestic too

-o-o-o-

~ Keep Calm and Carry Trays ~

Novelist *(Some Day My Prints Will Come)*

I'll write a book, I said with glee
You'll be amazed, it's up to me
The word is out, I'll have you know
… What wonders to you all I'll show

I'll add in verbs to be or not
And adjectives to paint the plot
How novel it is bound to prove
… A coffee first, then in my groove

Another coffee, it will come
The inspiration soon will run
The time line's critical no doubt
… A working lunch, then work it out

A chapter list, an index draft
Such preparation seems quite daft
"A mere two hundred words?" you say
… Tomorrow is another day

-o-o-o-

~ A Terrible Draft ~

Stevedore *(Water Affront)* *

The stevedores alas are gone
All made redundant one by one
Without a job since way back when
Containers took the place of men

Huge cranes lifting metric tonnes
The old days not passed down to sons
When men were handling smaller crates
All counted out in hundredweights

Close by bridges, down by Thames
Wonders of the world, such gems
Ropes a-lashing, nets a-swinging
Praises of the old trades singing

Upon the Thames down at the docks
The dockers off from wharfs have clocked

-o-o-o-

~ Quay Changes ~

Geography Teacher *(Give Them Latitude)* *

Now then class, prick up your ears
I've taught kids here for years and years
Learn well what I teach you then
And you'll get home quite safe again

The polar regions bite with frost
And jungles they can find you lost
Deserts will see you hallucinate
Your geo-learning to frustrate

There's many a place that's more than strange
While valleys rift and mountains range
Vast rivers often thunderous fall
Exploring may well need some balls...

So when exploring alien climes
Carry a ball of string betimes

-o-o-o-

~ Well Grounded ~

Fisherman *(101 Daft Notions)*

Sailing on the wildest oceans
A hundred of the daftest notions
Came to him as waking dreams
He wished them gone by any means

As on the seven seas he ranged
He thought the world to be so strange
These notions of all shapes and shades
Persisted pestering on parade

And trawling o'er horizons wide
He wished the notions cast aside
But couldn't shake off all those thoughts
The dreams are nightmares now of sorts

He'd gone out looking for some cod
Was not expecting he'd find God
Instead of notions come and gone
He now fights off a hundred and one

-o-o-o-

~ Fighting the Tide ~

Sewer Cleaner *(Basil's Jetting Ltd.)* *

An English idyll, made in Heaven
A lovely hamlet down in Devon
But when the sewers sprang a leak
All manner of things ran down the street

Now Basil owns a company
Jet-washing is his speciality
They called him out with swift intent
To deal with spilling effluent

His operatives they never shirked
Into the wee small hours they worked
Of obstacles they cleared the pipes
But lingering smells were rather ripe

When sweeter fragrances returned
The Council paid the cash well-earned

-o-o-o-

~ Feeling Flushed ~

Songwriter *(On the Beat)*

I'll sing you all the songs I know
And then one more before you go
I wrote them all myself in fact
This writing lark, I've got it cracked

I'll sing about the love we share
Cupid's dart is always there
And then there's politics and war
The subject list has so much more

The melodies, the bridge, the riffs
Are bound to see your spirits lift
Despite the doom and all life's gloom
A song will always light a room

So put a penny in my cap
I'm on the streets for all of that
I'll sing you songs as you pass by
And help your sorrows all to fly

-o-o-o-

~ Trouble Clef? ~

Deputy Speaker *(Woofer and Tweeter)* *

Order!, Order! I will shout
I'll sort the rowdy rabble out
The Speaker's off, he's rather tired
But I feel fresh, I'm fully wired

I'll stand no nonsense from front bench
They'll give way if they have some sense
They'd better watch the protocol
Best common-sense they must extol…

I've stood in for a day or two
The inmates think they're in a zoo
I just can't crack them, they're the pits
They're really getting on my… nerves

I'm worn out, it's a week by now
Come back Speaker, come back NOW!

-o-o-o-

~ Last Orders ~

Writer *(Seldom Wronger)*

She's an author and a writer
She's a lover and a fighter
She's a quibbler and a scribbler
She's a dabbler and a dribbler

She's oh so gripping, rarely trite
She's a dark one and a light
She's a thinker, intellectual
She's a ponderer and effectual

When pen to paper she does put
Her words well up right from the gut
Creating such imagined things
From paupers right on through to kings

Imaginings so wild she paints
Reality is what it ain't
The paupers all come out on top
While barbarous kings are for the drop

-o-o-o-

~ Pent-up Paper ~

Waitress *(Tipping the Balance)* *

For years I've served in café bars
Dreaming that I'd reach the stars
I've bag the stream of little tips
Now into savings I have dipped

I'm off on ventures round the world
With nature's wonders all unfurled
The cities and the towns of yore
Are beckoning on my Grand Tour

I've met a waiter in Cadiz
He's sent my head into a tizz
We are together, lives entwined
A better soulmate I'll not find

The best tip I can give to you
Is do the things you dream to do

-o-o-o-

~ Tea He! ~

Wedding Planner *(Weak Reception)* *

The film stars to each other said
'It's time that we pair must get wed
A wedding planner's what we need
A thousand guests we'll have to feed'

The planner was in great demand
Another project was in hand
A couple who had scrimped and saved
The simplest catering they craved

The invites sadly swapped around
The chaos did the stars confound
The rich pair got the cheaper deal
The other pair the champagne meal

If the stars they had foreseen
They might have plumped for Gretna Green

-o-o-o-

~ A Plight, to Tell the Troth ~

129

Botanist *(Leaf it Out)*

Some say she was a Satanist
'A Devil, she's no more than this'
In truth a botanist was she
Naming plants for me and thee

She named them indescribably
With tortuous taxonomy
With Latin words she just ran free
Naming plants for me and thee

Each kingdom had its own divisions
All neatly phylumed with precision
With genura and species see
Naming plants for me and thee

She gave up Latin in the end
Before she went right round the bend
She picked her grandma's brain it's true
Re-named the plants for me and you

-o-o-o-

~ The Root of the Matter ~

130

Boat Builder *(What a Funny Keeling)*

Of his vast ark protested Noah
'Will this odd project be a goer?
It's very well to float a craft
But all these animals... surely daft?'

'Bring more timber... two by two
Help me stack it... to me, to you
And when we're done 'neath sun and stars
We'll need more than a ha'porth of tar'

'The elephant and the kangaroo
Will tread upon the pigmy shrew
The tigers and the lions all
Will panic when hyenas call'

'You'd better Adam and Eve the snakes
Will slither thither, no mistake
The serpents too will all get out
Causing havoc, no slither of a doubt'

-o-o-o-

~ Noah More of This ~

131

Pub Landlady *(Boys Will Be Coy)*

In early days she was petite
And gently punters she would greet
But when two yobs came in to sup
She vowed to build her muscles up

She pulled the pints two at a time
Developed biceps by and by
Carted barrels in the cellar
Ready for unruly fellas

Then when the next time they came back
She grabbed the pair, their heads did crack
She told them 'If you don't act nice
You'll find out that you'll pay the price'

And from that day they were polite
Abstaining from the will to fight
She had no need to pull her punch
They ordered canapés for lunch

-o-o-o-

Schoolgirl *(Sneakiness and Slight)* *

Jane showed a flair for applied maths
But when it came to the swimming baths
They'd never ever pick poor Jane
Rose just laughed when the poor girl trained

Now when the maths exam came round
No higher marks than Jane's were found
With probability applied
Differentials were an easy ride

Computation was real fun
Her popularity though was none
Yet Head Prefect she soon was made
Her plans for the French vacation laid

And when it came to picking Rose
Jane said she'd rather pick her nose

-o-o-o-

~ Rose's Prospects ~

Schoolboy *(Ex Term Innate)* *

At fifteen Jim finds school a drag
Behind the bikesheds, crafty fag
His eager mates all egg him on
The Head arrives, they've upped and gone

He always gets the blame for things
Old Slasher's cane, it really stings
And as for writing out those lines
Detention? What a waste of time

He'll leave the town without a trace
As soon as he escapes this place
And heading off, no thought of school
He's sure to prove that he's no fool

For thanks to his unruly flair
He'll doubtless be a millionaire

-o-o-o-

~ Form Flinging ~

Explorer *(All Accordnance)*

The world is round, we all knew that
But not until we had a map
Explorers didn't have a clue
When sailing on the ocean blue

Columbus made a small mistake
On journeys he did undertake
Erroneous geography unfurled
For he'd perceived a smaller world

Vespucci he discovered ground
Embarked on such Amerigo round
The States of things in modern times
Are down to him and all his kind

And now we all have Google Earth
Definitive, for what it's worth
And so the world seems small once more
And yet more gross than times before?

-o-o-o-

~ Mappa Muddly ~

135

Astronaut *(Naught Better)*

The stars were always in his heart
Revering them right from the start
Castor one, another Pollux
He thought them all the very dog's bollocks

Serious is as Sirius does
Aldebaran and Betelgeuse
Polaris he ranked very high
Could never leave it from his sky

Rigel, Vega, Antares too
These were all his passion true
'Give me space man,' he would say
'It's the best thing any day'

Then one day he went up there
Disappeared into thin air
He never did come down again
Look up… he's passing now and then

-o-o-o-

~ The Sky's the Limit ~

Seamstress *(Buttonholed)* *

I knew a tailor in the past
He taught me much fine needlecraft
Such delicate work, I'll undergo
You'll be stitched up before you know

My stock of fabric and of thread
Will rule your heart if not your head
High is my skill and high my fee
My needlework's so sharp you see

I'll sew up things without a hitch
With my neatest blanket stitch
In dashing to my workshop mind
A running stitch you're bound to find

And if you fall when coming in
A slip stitch might be just the thing

-o-o-o-

~ *Hem Lion* ~

Chef *(Eat By Gum)*

The restaurant's opened up for lunch
The chef's so proud, as proud as Punch
A large man comes in through the door
He'd been for breakfast, now wants more

'I'll have each pudding listed here
Toute sweet too, I'll make it clear
I want them all, I'm so impressed
With chef's cuisine, it is the best'

'Service,' loudly calls the chef
The service waiter is so deft
The dishes dished up one by one
The large man's waistline is soon gone

He pays the bill, heads for the door
Calories loaded up for sure
Seven puddings he has scoffed
They have to take the door right off

-o-o-o-

~ Tort for Taut ~

Judge *(Bench Stench)*

He may be one of life's fair judges
Yet he attracts some mighty grudges
'Gaol me, would you?' says young Phil
'It's your fault, believing the Old Bill'

'I tell you straight, I wasn't there
I'm for the slammer, you don't care
They're lies, they're all fictitious links
This Court of Law it really stinks'

'It's so unfair, I've just been nobbled
The prosecution has been cobbled
I just can't say that I'll forgive
I know exactly where you live'

'I'm telling you, you're wrong again
My reputation's down the drain
And don't go calling me "my lad"
Even though you are my dad'

-o-o-o-

~ Just This for All ~

Mime Artist *(Silence is Gold, Then...)* *

I find it hard to speak to you
To tell you of the things I do
So I will just resort to mime
The imagery is quite divine

With vacant face and pure white gloves
Expression with my hands you'll love
Invisible barriers trapping me
I'm quizzical, you'll smile with glee

My hooped tee-shirt and black top hat
And blank expression tell you that
All consummate I play my part
My hands grasp at my fluttering heart

I did once scream though, I will say
When falling off a cliff one day

-o-o-o-

~ Nil by Mouth ~

Pharmacist *(Pillery Stocks) *

We've pills for this and pills for that
They'll make you thin, they'll make you fat
They'll calm your nerves when they're on edge
They'll render bald pates fully fledged

The doctor will prescribe the dose
A cure for illness always close
Order things upon your tablet
We will check and never scramble it

We'll grab you, jab you, puncture skin
Our services we'll boldly spin
A bandage here, a plaster there
You'll soon leave here without a care

But if you have too many ills
We have no anti-medicine pills

-o-o-o-

~ *Jab-a-wonky* ~

Wheelwright *(Bespoke)*

Proud of his historic art
His wheels were destined for a cart
But carts no longer were in vogue
The orders soon to be prorogued

'What can I do?' he asked despairing
'Other trades are better faring
Retrain, I think I really must
If not I surely will go bust'

So to the factory he went
Production targets all Hell-bent
Conveyor belts and robots too
Like much of most production do

Few and far now artisans
Even making pots and pans
Machines speak louder than those skills
Character it surely kills

-o-o-o-

~ What Goes Round… ~

Psephologist *(Poll De Rol)* *

Elections coming round again
The losers will the winners blame
But voting patterns I'll dissect
Results endeavouring to project

All Greek to me most of the time
With pebbles I'll the runes divine
Statistically I'll have you know
Just how the final vote should go

The populace will all know best
Though common-sense they oft divest
Majorities will call the day
The rest will call it unfair play

And when the outcome's opposite
I'll hide away and be contrite

-o-o-o-

~ Husting Away ~

Beachcomber *(Fortunate for Shore)*

He really was a sad old cove
Until the day he treasure trove
'Je l'ai trouvé,' he'd declared
'Eureka,' said in other word

He'd lived upon the sad seashore
Found poor cargo, not much more
Then in a bottle he found a deed
His ship came in, fortune indeed

He took the deed to legal minds
They told him 'keep what you did find
No other claim exists for this
Good fortune has you surely kissed'

'I can't believe I searched so long
For silver with my old mate John
The truest truth I now have found
I'll claim this cottage as my ground'

-o-o-o-

~ Drift He Would ~

Pirate *(Avast Avarice)* *

When Blackbeard found a shady cove
He asked the cove 'where is your trove?'
'X mark's the spot, I'm sure you knew
But what the eck's it to do with you?'

'If your map with me you'll share
We'll split the treasure, I declare'
'And if I don't, I'll have it all
Sharing makes no sense at all'

'But what about the pirate's code?
I want a half on me bestowed'
'Be off with you, I tell you now
I'll fire a shot across your bows'

And so they shot each other dead
Upon the quayside how they bled

-o-o-o-

~ Duel Control ~

Interior Designer *(The Fabric of Society)* *

Inside my head I make up schemes
To satisfy homeowners' dreams
To think them up on the exterior
Would surely turn out so inferior

I'm sure you'd like a purple patch
Orange and chocolate make a match
No reason and no rhyme its true
Perhaps I'd better chose a blue

My new blue colour scheme has legs
It is no joke, azure as eggs
And as for that limed-ash bookshelf
I must congratulate myself

When all is done, and dusted too
I'll think of something new for you

-o-o-o-

~ This Means Curtains ~

Barrister *(Flaw and Order)*

The barrister was off his head
'I'll have my day in court,' he said
'I'm just unbeatable I know
My case I'll win and fees will flow'

'When my client's in the dock
The evidence I will unlock
The jury will all side with me
He's innocent, they all will see'

He made such convoluted claims
At all costs win, it was his aim
The truth with him was economic
Thought by all as rather comic

'Take him down,' the Judge did sigh
'I've had enough of his damned lies
But let the poor accused go free
Lock up the lawyer, dump the key'

-o-o-o-

~ Court with His Trousers Down ~

Garden Gnome *(Still Life)* *

I sit here fishing, bored as Hell
There's no fish in this wishing well
But still I wish you well you know
As wandering by you come and go

I have to pose and smile all day
As you flit by upon your way
Those giant sparrows are a pest
And pigeon crap? Give me a rest

I dream of my own garden fair
Hat off, breezes in my hair
Rod put down and packed away
I'd love it every single day

And in a corner I would place
Some humans, each on their own base

-o-o-o-

~ Fish? Pish! ~

Civil Servant *(Serves 'em Right)* *

Boring days I work them through
And do my very best for you
At times I can't do right for wrong
I'd leave this job for half a song

My boss he gives me earache too
Insisting on what I must do
If he had half the nouse I've gained
He'd squander it, he's half a brain

I've always bit my poor old lip
And gave no lip, without a slip
Complete discretion always shown
Though the work is overblown

I'm leaving now, I'm out the door
I can't be civil anymore

-o-o-o-

~ Officious Business? ~

Sailor *(You're Barred My Lad)*

When first encountering Old Jack Tar
He'd travelled here from lands afar
He'd brought with him exotic wares
To sell on London's thoroughfares

Beyond the wharf he made his way
He left the docks without delay
Then wove his trade with silks so fine
And thought to tout his spice divine

But Excise men caught up with him
And took his booty on a whim
Small coin was all that he had asked
For arduous times before the mast

They took it all despite his pleas
He gave up riding on the seas
When last I met with Old Jack Tar
He was serving drinks at the harbour bar

-o-o-o-

~ A Bit of a Sea Shan't He... ~

Entomologist *(You Sixy Thing) **

All insects have six legs it seems
I've studied them since just sixteen
'Twas then the bug I truly caught
Without them my whole life is naught

I will not study spiders though
For they all have eight legs you know
And scorpions are not for me
Forget then arachnology

Now tiny mites are just the same
Too many legs, they're not my aim
And as for ticks? No way José
That bug won't bite me, 'go away!'

Insects are enough to list
With millions of them... get my gist?

-o-o-o-

~ Pull the Other One ~

Mountaineer *(The Height of Fashion)* *

She climbed the highest mountain see
On top of the whole world to be
O'er deep ravine and lofty pass
She'd dreamed of it since just a lass

The crampons really were a must
From base camp to the peak or bust
Her ice pick was the greatest boon
She felt like climbing to the moon

But thin up there was oxygen
She felt she must come down again
She found it hard to breathe the air
And didn't want to stay up there

But first she did secure a flag
From her posh Louis Vuitton bag

-o-o-o-

~ Roped Out of It ~

152

Optician *(Things Are Looking Up)*

She saw her way to earn a living
Helping folk with dodgy vision
They were so grateful I expect
So skilfully endowed with specs

But then did come the fateful day
Her keenness did just fade away
When she decided quite by whim
To turn to God and worship him

She teaches now religiously
Her pupils now see differently
They see the Lord so free and clear
Without the need for glasses near

And she's so glad to see the light
She proselytises day and night
And trusts her converts will stay true
Not detaching from her retinue

-o-o-o-

~ I Think I See the Light ~

University Don *(Dreaming Aspires)* *

When Donald passed the Eleven Plus
To grammar school, 'twas ever thus
And there he learned his subjects well
A genius, the truth to tell

Then taking all his Os and As
He realised that learning pays
To University he went
To learn some more he was Hell-bent

Now after many a studious year
He'd learned it all, or so he feared
'Can't go into the world,' he'd said
'My one true skill is being well-read'

So after some time staying on
Our Donald's now a Uni-Don

-o-o-o-

~ Sage's Ages ~

Naturist *(Bright and Freezy)* *

He found the beach all sheepishly
Stripped right off, jumped in the sea
He hoped the brine would soon refresh
When faced with such amounts of flesh

But when he felt the icy waters
Lapping round his nether quarters
He made a quick dash, that's for shore
The gathering breeze was rather raw

A gaggle of ladies did approach
Fresh unloaded from their coach
With sniggers and with titters… sadly
He ditched the bareness rather gladly

Now when to seaside he does go
He stays all wrapped from head to toe

-o-o-o-

~ Beach Bum ~

Stuntman *(A Tall Tale)*

He jumped with zest from chimneys high
Fast plummeting out of the sky
He'd felt compelled to do the stunt
While cardboard boxes took the brunt

Now Hollywood, they wanted more
More danger for the crowds to draw
So next he climbed a tall church spire
Then calmly dived into a fire

It all went wrong as it turns out
The camera crew they all did shout
'What a silly stunt,' they'd said
He spent three months confined to bed

Now some actors do their own tricks
But many end up using sticks
The years have passed for all, it's true
Our stuntman needs a stuntman too

-o-o-o-

~ Danger's Own ~

Pilot *(Fly Me to the Boon)*

The girl's given name was Violet
She was destined to become a pilot
But her schooling's no help there
It's left her career in the air

She still gained her wings quite soon
And she felt she could fly to the moon
But the holiday travellers all won
For *they* wished to fly to the sun

Though at high altitude she flew
Her passions fulfilled were but few
As sea levels continued to rise
They had to fit floats… quelle surprise

A seaplane is now in her charge
And holiday travel's at large
Folk now wish for trips by boat
And the cruise lines do naught but gloat

-o-o-o-

~ You Can't Always Jet What You Want ~

Holidaymaker *(Easter Gone West)* *

Everyone's on holiday
Travelling here and there today
The railway's engineering queues
Frustrating folk, promoting blues

The airports are clogged up again
Holiday flights going down the drain
While everyone is dressed in shorts
The ferries are stuck in the ports

The motorway's a real 'mare
The motorists don't have a prayer
The buses are all standing still
I think there might be time to kill

I guess I'll put my feet up here
And crack a bottle open… cheers!

-o-o-o-

~ Spring Broke ~

Comedian *(Funny, That)*

He thinks he's funny that's for sure
Jokes of bottoms and much more
Mentions Roger and Big Dick
His double entendres hard to lick

The old days' slander is no more
He can't insult his mother-in-law
Yet she can take it out on Fanny
Even if it insults granny

English, Irish, Scotsmen too
A joke on them just will not do
For sadly now, and here's the rub
Those men can't go into a pub?

So be careful what you say
The Comedy Police are on their way
Pour a drink, but just don't smoke
For laughter now… it is no joke

-o-o-o-

~ Mirth Dearth ~

Artist *(Hang it All)*

Which style of painting shall I pick?
Paint slapped on and daubed right thick?
Don't give a fig for Realism
I'll break away, I'll cause a schism

Abstract seems to suit me well
Though what it is, I just can't tell
Composition matters though
It soon attracts the real dough

My palate is for palettes wide
A dearth of colours I can't abide
And as for monochrome, oh no
Not that! I wouldn't stoop so low

Cubism, Pointillism, Surrealism too
But not just any old 'ism will do
I'm picky when all comes to all…
In choosing something for my wall

-o-o-o-

~ She Wants to Be Frameous ~

160

Wizard *(Spell Bound)* *

In days of old, fierce warlock I
A wizard now that time's gone by
Malevolent I was back then
I'm now benign I'll have you ken

I'm just like Father Christmas now
A knowing smile, a bushy brow
I bring kids gifts so magical
And hobbits see me as a pal

I'll fight all evil with panache
The darkest kingdoms, they will crash
I'll win the day for everyone
Cruel villains all will soon be gone

... This poor old wiz, how can it be?
Mere cinema's imprisoned me!

-o-o-o-

~ He's Been Framed ~

Racing Driver *(Car for the Course)* *

When he was just a little boy
They bought him motor-racing toys
With skid-lid and with goggles on
He set his sights on Formula One

'High octane fuel I'll burn at pace
I'll be a motor-racing ace
Even though the bends are tight
Chicanery will see me right'

But as for pole, he wasn't there
'It is the pits,' he did declare
'I'll catch them all, it's not in vain'
But then the clouds all shed their rain

At ninety plus he left the track
Wet-weather tyres still in the rack

-o-o-o-

~ Chicanery ~

Doctor *(G.P. Jeebies)*

His pulse is racing like a train
Such worries running through his brain
'Tell me, doctor. I'm not well?
My chips, I've had them, sure as Hell'

'Now, look my man, you are not ill
Of worriers I've had my fill
You're just a tad under the weather
Shake it! Pull yourself together'

'But nurse she filled me full of fear
She was surprised to see me here
She seemed to think that I was dead
Something that a neighbour said'

'Well I too thought you dead, it's true
I'd not seen hide nor hair of you
Get you home, you know it's best
Or else you'll clog the N.H.S.'

-o-o-o-

~ By Appointment ~

Property Developer *(A Weak Construct)* *

He's bought a run-down property
'I'll do it up for you and me
I'll take down the dividing walls
No need for trimming joists at all'

'And what are lintels? Pray do tell
Over windows? What the Hell
Forget a damp course too my dear
It hasn't rained that much this year'

'Mid-terrace is our territory
Nice and cosy we shall be
That open fire is so divine
No flue-lining will be just fine'

Without a doubt well-meaning but
He'll do it in, not do it up

-o-o-o-

~ Downright Guttered ~

Chemistry Teacher *(Safety Dearth)* *

Let's take some samples from the shelves
Their properties won't learn themselves
Now, see this Phosphorous my lads
We'll burn some, those fumes aren't that bad

Magnesium strip burns bright, you'll see
The loss of sight is temporary
Hydrogen, the sulphide kind
The smell of rotten eggs, divine

The quicksilver, that's Mercury
Upon your hand it runs so free
Sulphur, Lead, Plutonium too
That last one maybe's not for you

Sidney, do your laces up!
Untied they're dangerous, silly pup

-o-o-o-

~ Laced with Danger ~

Athlete *(Medal Mettle?)*

The years she's put in doing training
Even when it's heavy raining
Up the pole and round the track
In the pool both there and back

She's striving for a medal bold
Hoping for that cherished Gold
To match her sprinter husband Ron's
Though he came home with just a Bronze

The competition's ever tough
But she is made of sterner stuff
Until she goes and pulls a muscle
Ending her determined tussle

A Silver would have been enough
To stop her feeling quite so rough
But she knows deep down in her heart
It's winning... not the taking part

-o-o-o-

~ Pulling Power? ~

Street Performer *(Song and Dance Man)*

He once was in a famous band
Now stands alone with cap in hand
He dances all from dawn to dusk
Just wants to earn an honest crust

He knows the words to all the songs
And sings of righting life's great wrongs
The dances speak as strong as words
Of how the world is so absurd

Some will drop a coin or two
And listen to a verse right through
Others dance nimbler than he
To places where they need to be

At times a cheer is given birth
A few brief moments sharing mirth
His dog lays quiet, makes no fuss
At transient crowds all in a rush

-o-o-o-

~ Sing a Song of Sixth Sense ~

Astronomer *(Heaven's Above)*

She bought a brand new telescope
To spy on stars, or so she hoped
She set it on a tripod high
And pointed it up to the sky

The sky was at its darkest dark
The beauty at its starkest stark
How bright the firmament did seem
The canopy's ethereal dream

One night the strangest thing appeared
A saucer-shape earthward careered
A little man of greenest green
In the cockpit there was seen

He waved and smiled but then moved on
Flying skyward, off and gone
And now it's true she often sighs
He's never come back to her skies

-o-o-o-

~ Seeing Green ~

Surgeon *(A Time in Stitches)*

He was a cut above the rest
They all agreed he was the best
He'd operate with laugh and grin
Oh, the stitches he had them in

Of course he dressed so fine and neat
He really scrubbed up quite a treat
With patients he would joke and quip
While they were hooked up to their drip

He always worked the longest shifts
The nitrous oxide he would sniff
They found his voice a real gas
But away he floated, alack alas

They found him later far away
He'd landed in a stack of hay
All complete with gloves and gown
But stitching needle never found

-o-o-o-

~ Suture Self ~

Headmaster *(Old's Cool)* *

My father was an Eton mess
We didn't speak, I must confess
When I was young, impressionable
No repartee, t'was rather dull

So that's why I became self-taught
The learning bug it had me caught
I passed on girls, but passed exams
And then I swotted on the Cam

With gown and mortarboard I reign
I'm like a king in my domain
I wielded cane with fabled zest
Until they told me 'give it best'

And now the kids just won't sit quiet
Say teachers 'They're just running riot'

-o-o-o-

~ Cane and Fabled ~

Witch *(Black to the Dark Ages)* *

I've told them I'm a white witch true
They don't believe me, but do you?
I've never harmed a single soul
My sister though acts black as coal

I never should have took from her
The broomstick hid beneath the stair
As for the cat? It hitched a ride
Beneath my cloak the beast did hide

The cauldron? not a good look, right
I was merely cooking supper that night
They've tied me up the stupid fools
And brought out their old ducking stool

I might as well wear black from now
Malicious spells? I'll show them how

-o-o-o-

~ Spelled Out ~

Weather Presenter *(The Sky's the Limit)*

The Earth it spins and daylight comes
I've worked it out, I've done the sums
The weather map it's all off pat
With caveats for all of that

Capricious always weather is
But nonetheless, I've done the biz
So fickle is the climate now
But I have fathomed it somehow

I must convince you that it's true
Give certainty for me and you
I ponder it all through the night
And sometimes I can get it right

So take your brolly if it's fine
Or putting dryness on the line
Leave your brolly on the shelf
And if it's raining... please yourself

-o-o-o-

~ Meteorology Rains, Okay ~

Woodwork Teacher *(Kit-astrophe?)* *

Remember you lot… 'safety-first!'
So do your best, don't do your worst
I'm here to see you all behave
The planes alone are for close shaves

When sawing keep you free hand wide
Or else a glove, don't let it slide
And tape measures can spring right back
They'll have an eye out just like that

The drills are high speed tools, beware
They'll easily tangle in long hair
Keep hands behind the chisel blades
Or else you'll need some swift first-aid

The first time Johnny's safety cracked
The board-rubber, his head it thwacked

-o-o-o-

~ Rebating On ~

Chauffeuse *(Wheely Fast)*

'Take me to the Ritz, my man
Make it speedy if you can
I wish to meet investor Don
And if I'm late he will be gone'

'Right away sir that I'll do
But I'm a woman through and through
Remember when you employed me
The long gold locks were there to see'

'This uniform was meant for guys
The cap my gender does disguise
But like the bloke you fired last week
I'll step on it… a fast blue streak'

And when the toff he did arrive
Quaking feebly from the drive
Dear old Don was not impressed
Deciding he would not invest

-o-o-o-

~ In Top Gear ~

Station Guard *(Sleeper Creeper)*

The train that stands at platform nine
Unusually is right on time
Dragon-like the engine steams
The station guard of home he dreams

His hunter watch he now consults
And blows his whistle for results
His neat green flag he briskly waves
Then homeward bound, he supper craves

Once the train has been and gone
He puts his trusty bike clips on
With a leap his crossbar straddles
No stopping him, away he pedals

Once he's suppered, quite replete
He needs to rest his weary feet
Puts on slippers, ditching shoes
On the right track for a snooze

-o-o-o-

~ All Puffed Out ~

Electrician *(Shocking Behaviour)*

A live performance he prefers
To switch the mains off seems absurd
He insulates his favourite snips
Consumer unit… still it trips

Regardless, pliers he employs
His radio blurts out such noise
His methods are not down to earth
He's been that way right since his birth

The ring-main now he does connect
Spurred on, still being too direct
He's neutralising common sense
A shock would send him swiftly hence

He's got his rubber wellies on
Otherwise he might be gone
Ignoring danger that he brings
Our Sparks might fly, and gain his wings

-o-o-o-

~ Terminal? ~

Fashion Designer *(Wear With All)* *

Fashion gurus through the years
Garb for those contemporary peers
The family tree reveals it all
Our stock-in-trade has clothed them all

Designing Macaroni wigs
For bourgeoisie all seen as prigs
Later, dandys had their day
Flamboyancy still holding sway

Stovepipe hats and waistcoats too
Cloche hats, berets just for you
Kaftans, dungarees and flairs
What ever next, we stand prepared

And years before in Stone Age times
Our forebears bearskins they designed

-o-o-o-

~ Material Change ~

Carpenter-Joiner *(Against the Grain)*

At first a carpenter at best
A joiner soon with more finesse
A table there a cupboard here
Carving out a real career

Grinling Gibbons was his name
His work soon shot him into fame
And later both the Chippendales
With their fine act just couldn't fail

In the meantime Hepplewhite
Made chairs and things, his prospects bright
So many names we're furnished with
What more pleasure could they give?

And later, now poor Grinling's gone
He'd carved rich fruits with leaves upon
Intricate bows and delicate ribbons
Inevitably now a dwindling Gibbons

-o-o-o-

~ What a Relief ~

Car Mechanic *(Classy Chassis)*

He's underneath the bonnet diving
So as to keep his business thriving
Changing plugs and rotor arm
Those old cars are full of charm

'Computers, no!' He can't be doing
With all the gadgets thence ensuing
While cars on that there 'tricity
He can't abide them, can't you see

An oil pressure gauge is cool
A voltmeter among his tools
Indicator arms are charming
Cranking handles so disarming

Grease guns, who could want for more
And Haynes manuals he loves for sure
The newer cars make him so sad
With old ones pleasure can be had

-o-o-o-

~ Attention Spanner ~

Charity Worker *(Pay-back Time)* *

I'm in the shop down High Street way
My job is such a giveaway
You give me all your bric-a-brac
Sometimes good but often tat

I'll sell it on to someone else
They'll put it on a waiting shelf
They'll dust it every Saturday morn
But years from now it'll be a yawn

They'll bring it back to give to me
Recycled to the nth degree
A hundred years of come and go
The roundabout of human woe

It's such a convoluted path
When up front we could just give cash

-o-o-o-

~ Roundabout Time ~

Nurse *(Well Intentioned)* *

On hospital wards she keenly worked
From crucial duties never shirked
The ever-filling six-bed bays
Occupied each working day

Amid the drips she soon did learn
Some 'patients' oft defied the term
'Virtue' not within their vocab
Especially those just in for rehab

Now many times she bit her lip
Yet never did she lose her grip
With ever-present patient smile
She'd always go the extra mile

But one day after several glitches
She had her patients all in stitches

-o-o-o-

~ On Wards and Upwards ~

Baby *(Me, Myself, Sigh)* *

I ventured out at forty weeks
To learn a few things, so to speak
The wonders of the world so stunning
All life upon the planet thrumming

The subtle balance of all things
There is no doubt the planet sings
The mountains, valleys and the seas
What wonders grow in all of these

Then come the day when we arrived
At first allowing things to thrive
We let our actions start to jade it
And balance soon forlorn it faded

From darkness into light back then
I think I'll go back in again

-o-o-o-

~ Difficult Berth ~

Potter *(Fired with Enthusiasm)*

Harriet was a potter sure
Wizard at her craft and more
Punters at her market stall
Were truly spellbound, one and all

On potters' wheel she never faded
Enthusiasm was never jaded
The slip-glaze she applied with skill
Her bulging order book to fill

Her kiln craft sure was all-inspiring
Jars and vases ever firing
People came from far and wide
And bought the pots with real pride

There was one jar exceeding big
A master piece with heavy lid
She climbed inside and slept so tired
A shame the kiln then auto-fired

-o-o-o-

~ Obliviate! ~

Driving Examiner *(Emergency Start)*

His parking isn't parallel
He thinks he's on a carousel
Don't ask about his three-point-turn
The Highway Code? He's not concerned

This is his thirty-second test
And doomed it is like all the rest
He sticks at it I'll give him that
But he's exceeded all the stats

For me to pass him I'd be mad
I've never seen one quite so bad
And let loose on the Motorway
All discipline would go astray

To him the Mirror is a paper
A signal just a pointless caper
Manoeuvre board! I'm jumping ship
I'll just resign before I flip

-o-o-o-

~ Hell Plates ~

Chip Shop Owner *(Fission Chips)* *

He doesn't take his chip shop lightly
Opens up for seven days… nightly
The fish is freshly caught at sea
A tasty treat for you and me

He's ordered a 'new clear' sign
Encouraging more folk to dine
Perhaps the menu has weird scope
Is he selling isotopes?

His promo is intense and tireless
With advertising on the wireless
But radio activity
Is not that wise, he just can't see

Yet once folk all have tasted some
It goes down swift… just like a bomb

-o-o-o-

~ Good Cod ~

Horticulturist *(Home Groan)* *

All good things stem from the soil
Aided by the farmers' toil
At least that's just the way things were
Before the D.N.A. was stirred

Now with modified genetics
Oft for flimflam or aesthetics
Cutlets masquerade as meat
It's nuts for our taste buds to cheat

While feeding people is the aim
Making dosh is oft the game
Cultivating plants for food
Needs producers to be shrewd

So to the market food to bring
Haughty culture is the thing

-o-o-o-

~ Plant Biased Food? ~

Minstrel *(That Sing King Feeling)*

'Who will sing a melody
To lift me from my misery?'
King John declared this plaintively
He'd lost his crown upon the sea

'This melancholy will not stand
With my fair music close at hand
I'll sing a melody so sweet
Your gloom I'm sure we'll soon defeat'

'Woe betide your tide of woe
We're bound to trump Canute you know
We'll turn the tide on all your sorrow
Things look good for your tomorrow'

And so his musical refrain
Sent darkling thoughts straight down the drain
Such sadness proved a load of tosh
The crown it came out in The Wash

-o-o-o-

~ Singing for His Scupper ~

French Teacher *(A Rough Translation)* *

'Please miss, quickly, I must use the loo?
I'll burst if I don't, I'll relax if I do'
'Of course you may Tim, *mais oui* you may pee
You must hurry now or your pee we'll all see'

'*Merci*, a mercy trip I certain do need
I just couldn't face it if too soon I wee'd'
'*Non, merci vous*, Tim, or perhaps *merci tu*
Though *tu's* rather intimate really for you'

'Today, *auxjourd'hui* miss I just have to leak
A path to the toilet, I'll urgently seek'
'Begone to the *pissoir*, don't piss on our floor
J'espère, I do hope you can get to the door'

'*Une mer de urine*? *Ma mère* would think '*Merde*'
I couldn't go home miss, I just wouldn't dare'

-o-o-o-

~ The School Run ~

Stagehand *(Interval)* *

He treads the boards between each act
But heavy scenery brings bad backs
Alas, poor Eric went off sick
A few days' rest would do the trick

His wife she drew the curtains close
Ensured that Eric was well dosed
To him there is a lot at stake
At least a leg he didn't break

He'd worked the stage for many years
Laughed a lot and shed some tears
He felt he must his role reprise
With comedies and tragedies

He's back on stage in just a week
And playing his part... so to speak

-o-o-o-

~ Stage... Left ~

189

Clown *(All Made Up)*

Some say 'Oh, he's rather vile
Underneath the painted smile
Fills his long boots with scrunched paper
Then performs such facile capers'

His baggy pants were once quite smart
His flower squirting from the heart
Although his little car is dopey
His big top once was not so ropey

He gets upset if folk don't cheer
The boisterous laughs he longs to hear
Deep down he is just like us all
Still hoping for good fortune's call

Now he's retired from the scene
The kids have grown, they're nowhere seen
He sits and dreams on trailer steps
The memories well up from the depths

-o-o-o-

~ All Made Up ~

Bookbinder *(A Page From History)*

Back in the seventeenth century
A bloke went on a killing spree
Matthew Hopkins was his name
Witchfinder was his claim to fame

He sought them here, he sought them there
But naught was clear, and naught was fair
Bookbinder Fred then undertook
To hunt him down, bring him to book

Fred found the largest book he could
For cover and spine used heavy wood
He made it nice with marbled papers
'I'll put an end to all his capers'

He found the Finder in a trice
Hopkins paid the fatal price
What a bind the book did prove
For Hopkins' head was badly grooved

-o-o-o-

~ Ex Libris ~

Archaeologist *(Futurehistoric)*

Delving deep he sure did dig it
Unearthing history, up did big it
Telling tales of pots and kilns
In damp valleys, on bleak hills

A trowel and sieve his only tools
Abiding always by old rules
Detectorists he frowned upon
Said 'Custom true is past and gone'

Then one day when he dug right deep
He thought he heard the faintest beep
An ancient spaceship he'd disturbed
And off it flew just like a bird

And now he sits all day entranced
The olden days just mere romance
The past is future, future's passed
That trench he'd dug had proved his last

-o-o-o-

~ If You're in a Hole… ~

Barber *(Cutting Room Floor)*

'I'd better trim your hair,' he said
'If not, upon it you will tread
It must be many years it's grown?'
'Since Queen Victoria took the throne'

'And since I have a beard right fair
You can wield your scissors there'
'I will, my man, you'll be refreshed
Without this hair that's so enmeshed'

The barber cut and cut away
As if it were his final day
He nicked his neck and red blood flew
'Fear not I am a surgeon too'

He bound him up in bandage white
But sadly wound it rather tight
Now with the cut hair on the floor
A body lies… he is no more

-o-o-o-

~ Cutting Hair No Longer, But Shorter ~

Jockey *(The Going's Hard)* *

Diminutive he's bound to be
Beyond the jumps he cannot see
Unless he's on his champing steed
When twenty hands he well exceeds

The starting pistol sounded loud
Waking wide expectant crowd
The cheers and whoops all filled his ears
Dispelling all his trepid fears

But dear old Dobbin did respond
Of such loud noise he wasn't fond
Like a bullet off he went
The distant spire was his intent

The jockey's zest was not to be
The point-to-point he couldn't see

-o-o-o-

~ Saddles with It ~

Alchemist *(Lab Oratory)* *

I seek the Stone of Knowledge pure
A panacea, disease to cure
Elixir for immortal life
No more anguish, no more strife

Base metal I will turn to gold
My goal is nothing if not bold
I'll find eternal health and youth
I'll live a life of peace and truth

The Stone once found will sow the seeds
The chemistry is all it needs
Though people see me as a geek
Philosophy will make it speak

And when there's nothing left to find
I'll turn to crosswords, test my mind

-o-o-o-

~ Base Mettle ~

Soldier *(Combat Fatigue)* *

I'd thought to join the army when
The Government had wanted men
The world in pointless fresh turmoil
On trouble waters pouring oil

The thought of battle brings despair
But someone has to be right there
To help stop madness of conflict
When war's the option that's been picked

The world with all it's wonders fair
Is put on hold when war's declared
So much to lose, so must I choose?
Can no one now snuff out the fuse?

And when the fighting's been and gone
The world will sing a hollow song

-o-o-o-

~ War to the Point ~

Tattoo Artist *(Beauty's Only...)*

Admirers of this strangest art
Black and blue right from the start
I'll ink you 'til the pigments drown
Come inside and sit you down

There's dolphins, dragons, skulls and bones
Kings and queens upon their thrones
I'll cover all; arms, legs and face
No surface missed, no hiding place

Every surface is fair game
I'll ink you with your partner's name
Inside and out, above, below
Ink you where no man should go

When all is done you'll look so frightening
Specially with that dental whitening
Your friends will only recognise
The precious sparkle in your eyes

-o-o-o-

~ By The Skin of Your Teeth ~

Animator *(A Filmsy Excuse?)* *

Bugs Bunny was a favourite target
What a gift, an instant market
But he was framed, they all do say
Twelve pairs a second was the way

Armed with pencil 'Verithin'
To use a keyboard seemed a sin
Tom's mouse is not called Gerry now
I guess it's not the same somehow

He's hung up his old drawing board
His hand-drawn sketches are all stored
For sure it was a sad, sad day
His brush with paint now packed away

Digital has muscled in
Popeye's spinach in the bin

-o-o-o-

~ Framed ~

Blacksmith *(Can't Say Farrier Than That)*

Of iron hot my trade is wrought
I took to it without a thought
But someone said it's plain to see
It's nothing more than forgery

And so I turned to horses' hooves
A farrier I might better prove
Upon the anvil hammer sat
I couldn't be ferrous than that

With horses nothing dubious be
Just four feet, naught more can we see
But four-feet-nought is just twelve hands
That's how tall this pony stands

What more is there, what better cause
Than help a horse perform his chores?
Forget the weathervanes and such
Without him life's not worth so much

-o-o-o-

~ Shoe Some Emotion ~

Numismatist *(Spent by Pennies)*

Back in his early spendthrift days
He'd 'loads o' dosh' to coin a phrase
But then he started hoarding money
Not spending any, oh how funny

'There's nowt in notes,' he'd say to friends
'Coins are the only means to ends'
The ends he meant were collecting them
And henceforth all his troubles stemmed

He took collecting to extremes
The coins they filled his every dream
They also filled his every room
Imprisoning him as in a tomb

A nightmare it had all become
They found him buried, overcome
They never heard his desperate calls
Coins proved the root of evils all

-o-o-o-

~ Bit by Coins ~

ALL OUT

~

The End

200 ~ Declared ~ *Poems on the Run*

Alphabetical Index:

Printed in Great Britain
by Amazon